Collins gem

Ga
Trees

Keith Rushforth

First published in 2005 by Collins,
an imprint of HarperCollinsPublishers
77-85 Fulham Palace Road, London W6 8JB
www.collins.co.uk

Text © Keith Rushforth
Artworks and design © HarperCollinsPublishers
Photography by Tim Sandall and Keith Rushforth
Based on material from the Collins Practical Gardener series

Project Editor: Claire Musters
Designer: Helen McTeer
Indexer: Kathy Steer

For HarperCollins:

Senior Managing Editor: Angela Newton
Editor: Alastair Laing
Assistant Editor: Lisa John

A CIP catalogue record for this book is available
from the British Library

ISBN 0 00 720441 8

Colour reproduction by Digital Imaging

Printed and bound by Amadeus S.r.l., Italy

CONTENTS

HOW TO USE THIS BOOK

This book is divided into two parts. The first chapter guides you through the basic care of trees. The majority of the book is given over to the plant directory, which provides individual entries on the best tree species to grow, listed alphabetically by Latin name. The example entry below is annotated to show you what information each section provides.

The Latin name of the plant, followed by its common name where relevant

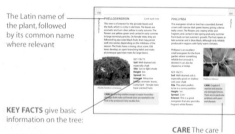

KEY FACTS give basic information on the tree:

Soil: the best soil to grow the plant in
Site: whether to plant in a sunny or shady position
Height: the average height of popular garden varieties after 10 years
Spread: the average spread of popular garden varieties after 10 years
Interest: indicates why the plant is grown – such as for its flowers, foliage etc

CARE The care box gives specific information on feeding and pruning requirements as well as indicating what pests and diseases the plant is prone to

INTRODUCTION

The main reason for having trees in the garden is for their display of foliage. This can take on a bewildering array of shapes and sizes and may also provide great seasonal colour. Flowers, fruit and bark on many trees add inspirational colour and interest to a garden throughout the year too. A few trees are also grown for the exquisite scent they produce. Given their size and permanence, trees will often provide form and structure in a garden, which means that the shape or habit of each one is very important as well.

As you can see, trees provide a wealth of interest in gardens and this book offers you all the information you need on a large selection of the top specimens. Armed with its thoroughly practical advice, you will be able to enjoy your chosen garden trees throughout the year.

CARING FOR GARDEN TREES

This chapter gives you all the information and advice you need to choose and care for garden trees.

GROWING CONDITIONS

Before you buy any plants, it is important to assess the type of garden you have.

Aspect and exposure

Does your garden face north, south, east or west? This affects which parts will get the most, or least, sun. The degree of exposure that your garden experiences is another determining factor in what plants will grow.

Soil

Each type of soil can vary greatly in drainage capacity, fertility and chemical composition. Soils can be alkaline, acidic or neutral (pH testing kits are available from garden centres) but each type can be improved by the addition of organic matter.

Syringa vulgaris likes alkaline soils.

SOIL PREPARATION

Before buying and planting any trees, make sure the soil is in as good a condition as possible.

Compacted soil

Trees cannot grow in compacted soil. If you discover you have compacted soil you will need to remove about two fork depths of soil, break up the subsoil underneath with a pickaxe then replace the topsoil.

Waterlogging

Waterlogged soil can kill a plant by drowning the roots. It is often caused by compaction or poorly draining soils – such as clay. With such soils, digging in organic matter and applying a layer of organic mulch will help to improve drainage.

Weeds

Control weeds before planting to ensure new plants are not competing for nutrients. Larger weeds can be removed by hand or by forking over the soil. Perennial weeds need treatment with a chemical weedkiller.

TIP: If you dislike using chemicals, you could try laying sheet mulches for several weeks or months before planting to kill off the weeds or use an organic mulch (*see* p. 15).

CHOOSING AND BUYING TREES

Trees come in a wide range of shapes and sizes. Creating the effect you want in the garden requires careful consideration.

Selecting your plants

Few trees are in flower or fruit for more than a couple of weeks a year so the form of each tree, and the eventual height and spread it will achieve when mature, are equally important.

Once you have decided on the basic forms you prefer, the next stage is to draw up some design ideas for how to incorporate trees into the overall scheme. Apart from their decorative features, trees can be planted as hedging or screening, to mark out areas of the garden and to give shade and shelter.

Buying trees

Trees can be bought from a variety of sources – garden centres, general and local nurseries, and specialist nurseries – and are available as container-grown, bare-rooted or rootballed.

CONTAINER-GROWN PLANTS

Plants grown in containers have their root system intact, which means they should thrive when planted out. The main drawback is that container-grown trees can become 'potbound' if left for too long. With potbound plants you will find the roots have filled the container and started to find a way out; such plants are unlikely to establish a new root system when they are planted out.

BARE-ROOTED PLANTS

Bare-rooted trees weigh much less than container plants so are easier to transport. The main drawback is that much of the root system is left in the nursery soil, which means they can be slow to establish in a new position.

ROOTBALLED PLANTS

Rootballed trees are nursery-grown plants that have been lifted with the soil still attached to the roots. To stop the soil falling off, which would cause the roots to dry out, the ball of soil is wrapped in hessian or a coarse cloth. For some items, buying a rootballed tree is a good compromise between the relative cheapness of bare-rooted stock and the expense of container-grown plants.

PLANTING TECHNIQUES

No tree likes to be planted deeper than it has been growing. Always plant at the soil mark on the stem made by the nursery soil or at the level of the container. If in doubt, plant on the shallow side.

Container-grown plants

Before planting container-grown plants, trim back any damaged top portions to good shoots and check to see if the compost has dried out. If it has, leave it to soak in a bucket of water for an hour or two. Do not leave it soaking too long or you will kill all the fine roots. Container-grown stock can be planted at any time of the year, but if planted during the summer months will require regular watering.

To plant a container-grown tree Dig a hole of the correct depth but ensure it is at least 5cm (2in) wider than the container. Remove the tree from its pot. If the roots have formed a circular mass in the bottom of the pot, tease them out so they spread as widely as possible. If there are woody circling roots that cannot be teased out, cut them with secateurs at three points equally spaced around the circle to allow new roots to form. This will prevent the roots growing in a circling manner (trees with such roots usually end up blowing over). Replace the soil in layers no more than

10–15cm (4–6in) thick. Firm each layer with the ball or toes of your feet but avoid firming with the heel (as this will almost certainly cause compaction of the soil).

Planting a hedge

Spacing of hedging plants will depend upon how long you can wait for the hedge to thicken and what its purpose is – a hedge intended to keep animals in (or out) will need stems closer together than a purely visual hedge. Generally, spacings of between 0.5m (1½ft) and 1m (3ft) are suitable. For a thicker hedge, double plant with two alternating rows.

Bare-rooted plants

Bare-rooted trees should only be planted when dormant, between late autumn and early spring. If in leaf, the plant will not be able to absorb enough water to compensate for the loss of roots. If the roots are dry, soak them in a bucket of water for up to 12 hours.

To plant a bare-rooted tree Dig the hole to the correct dimensions to hold the roots. Make sure that the hole is even and dug to the correct depth, that is, dig no deeper than the level it was planted in the nursery (1). If any roots are bent so that they are growing into the centre of the plant, bend them back outwards. If this cannot be done, prune them off, otherwise you risk the bent roots girdling the other roots and causing the tree to blow over in the future. Backfill around the roots (2), firming as you go but taking care not to compact the soil. Tie up to a stake if necessary (*see* opposite page).

1 Dig a hole no deeper than the level the tree was growing at.

2 Once the plant is in position, backfill around the roots.

Rootballed plants

Rootballed trees can be planted over a longer period than bare-rooted ones, but avoid late spring to early autumn. Check the condition of the soil. Fibrous-rooted plants can be soaked if dry, but many rootballed specimens have coarser root systems that will fall apart if wetted. These are best watered in after planting. Trim back damaged top portions to good shoots.

To plant a rootballed tree Dig a hole to the same depth as the rootball, but 5cm (2in) wider to allow for the roots. Place the plant in the centre of the hole and untie or cut the wrapping. Do not remove this – spread it out in the bottom of the hole, where it can be left to rot down.

Untie the wrapping, leaving it in the hole.

Tease out any roots that are free from the soil of the rootball and bend back or cut off any girdling or circling roots. Backfill with soil in layers of 10–15cm (4–6in) thick, firming as you go. Stake if necessary.

Staking

Newly planted trees often need staking. A stake holds the roots firm so that the brittle feeder roots are not damaged by the plant rocking in the wind. There should be no more than 5cm (2in) of stake above the tie; otherwise in windy weather the stem will flex and rub against the stake. Use a thin batten, which allows more flexibility. Tie it in with tape rather than wire or twine, which would cut into the stem.

TIP: Once the fine roots have become woody, a tree should not need further staking. A small tree should be staked for up to a year, and a larger tree for up to two years.

TRANSPLANTING

Moving established plants can be a way of keeping specimens that do not fit into the new design in their existing positions. Small plants, less than 1m (3ft) can easily be dug with a spade and moved bare root, as they will not make adequate rootballs. Larger plants that have reached at least 2m (6½ft) in height, can be moved with a rootball.

Transplanting a mature tree requires real care. First, make a guideline around the plant, digging a vertical slit a minimum of 30cm (1ft) from the stem (or 50–60cm [1⅔–2ft] for trees that are 3–4m [10–13ft] high). Remove a spadeful of soil from outside the guideline, working around the plant to dig a trench between 30–50cm (12–20in) deep. Next, use the spade to cut horizontally across from the base of the trench, freeing the tree from the soil. Gently rock it to one side and slip a folded sheet of polythene beneath the rootball. Rock the plant to pull the sheet out at the far side. Then either lift the plant or dig a ramp on one side and drag it to its new position. Replant as for a new rootballed plant.

TIP: It is generally best to transplant during the dormant season – from late autumn to early spring.

MULCHING

A mulch is a layer of material applied to the ground around plants to conserve moisture, suppress weeds and maintain an even temperature.

Organic mulches

These include bark and wood chippings, as well as those with a high nutrient content – peat, peat-substitutes, leafmould and manure.

Inert mulches

The two main types are pea gravel and synthetic sheeting. Sheet mulches allow water to percolate through while reducing evaporation from the surface.

Laying sheet mulches Use a full sheet to cover a whole bed. Lay it before planting but after soil preparation. Mark the positions of the trees on the sheet and cut a cross for each one. Fold back the four flaps and plant through the centre, laying the flaps back around afterwards. For a specimen tree, lay an individual square of sheeting around the base, cutting a slit to ensure it is wrapped right round the plant.

Cut a cross in the sheet for each plant.

FEEDING AND WATERING

Although trees generally do not require much feeding it is vital to provide enough food and water when they are newly planted.

Feeding

If your soil is poor, apply a mulch of well-rotted manure or leafmould at the rate of a wheelbarrow load for every 3sq m (3½sq yd). Unless your plants are showing specific signs of nutrient deficiency, apply a balanced general fertiliser at a rate of 60g (2oz) per 1m sq (1yd sq) each spring.

Watering

Moisture requirements are covered in the individual plant entries, but generally most trees require regular watering during the growing season in the first year after planting in order to get established quickly.

Little water is needed during the winter months. The amount needed during summer increases with the strength of the sun. However, the other factor you must consider is the water-holding capacity of the soil you are planting into.

Regular watering helps newly planted trees to get established.

PRUNING

The main reasons for pruning are to control the size of the plant and the direction of growth, to tidy up the branch structure, to maximise flowering displays or to promote new growth.

Equipment

Secateurs A pair of secateurs will cut through shoots up to 1cm (½in) thick and is the best tool for most pruning of small trees. Secateurs come in two styles. By-pass secateurs have a sharp blade and a blunt blade, which cut by a scissor action. With anvil secateurs the sharp blade cuts against the middle of a blunt anvil. By-pass secateurs cause less bruising to the shoot and are better for finer pruning, whereas anvil secateurs will cut thicker shoots.

Shears Useful for trimming hedges. Choose shears that have a notch in one blade near the base as these make cutting woody stems easier.

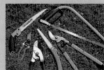

Saws Use a pruning saw to remove branches from established trees. A bowsaw is useful for cutting through larger branches.

Secateurs, shears and saws handle progressive degrees of pruning.

Fine pruning

Pruning current or one-year wood requires fine cuts. Make the cut about 0.5cm (¼in) above a bud or pair of buds from which new shoots will grow. Where there are opposing buds, cut straight across the stem; where there are alternate buds, cut at an angle. Choose buds that will grow outwards, so that the plant develops an open framework of branches. For cuts into larger stems, where regrowth will be from dormant buds, make the cut at an angle so that water drains off the cut surface.

Cut diagonally into larger stems.

Removing a branch

To avoid making a tear that runs down the stem and rips the bark off, make the cut in three stages for branches over 15cm (6in). Make an under cut upwards through the branch at a point about 30cm (1ft) from where you wish to remove the branch, only cutting to about a quarter of the thickness of the branch. Next make a cut from the top of the branch 2.5cm (1in) beyond the first cut. When you are about halfway through the branch it should snap off without a tear. This leaves a short stump or 'snag' that is much easier to remove with a final single cut. On smaller branches less than 15cm (6in), make two cuts above and below, which will give a neat cut.

Most trees have special defences for healing the wounds left after a branch has been removed, but for these to come into play the final cut must leave the collar intact around the base of the branch. This collar is thicker on the trunk side than on the branch side and is normally at an angle across the branch, nearer the trunk at the top and further away at the bottom. Therefore make the final cut at a point on the branch beyond the edge of the collar, angling the saw slightly so that the cut slopes away from the trunk.

TIP: When removing a branch from a tree always put safety first. Do not use a chainsaw above chest height under any circumstances. If you cannot remove the branch with a 60cm (2ft) bowsaw, then employ a professional.

Training

This is the simplest form of pruning. With established trees, training involves cutting back a plant that has become too large or has spread in the 'wrong' direction. General maintenance to remove dead, defective or crossing limbs is part of training. Errant branches should be removed either where the branch originates on the stem, or at a side branch or bud.

Most newly planted trees will also require some initial training to promote vigorous growth and a balanced, open shape. After planting, prune back any dead, damaged or crossing stems and thin out if necessary.

Coppicing and pollarding

With trees that have grown too large, one option is to cut them back hard to just above ground level, a technique known as 'coppicing'. This is a quick way both to reduce and rejuvenate a plant. Pollarding is a variant of coppicing; the main difference is that a pollard has a stem, often 2.4–5m (8–16½ft) in height. To coppice a tree, cut it down to between 5–15cm (2–6in) above ground level. You may need to thin out the new growth after the first season to form a natural shape. Coppicing is best carried out in spring.

Pollarding involves cutting the overgrown branches of a tree back to leave a stem.

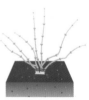

Coppicing involves cutting a tree back to just above ground level.

TIP: Only trees that regrow from dormant buds in the bark can be coppiced. Most conifers will die if cut back hard.

Pruning a mature tree

If you need to keep a larger tree within bounds, remove surplus branches – cutting them off where they join the trunk or main stems so as not to leave a 'snag'. Shorten longer branches by cutting off the larger portion where there is a side branch or fork.

Pruning to flower

Pruning is also carried out to increase flowering. There are two main categories for this type of pruning and knowing which one you are dealing with can make all the difference between impressive floral displays and undistinguished foliage.

The difference between the two groups is whether they flower from buds laid down last year (Group 1) or whether they flower on new growth (Group 2). Generally, Group 1 trees and shrubs flower over winter, in spring or early summer, while Group 2 plants flower in summer and autumn.

Group 1 These plants should be pruned immediately after they finish flowering. In general, restrict pruning to the older shoots, leaving the newer shoots intact, as they tend to flower better on the spur shoots that are formed in the second year of a stem's life.

Group 2 These plants can be hard pruned just as growth is starting in the spring, which will encourage them to make vigorous new growths that will bear the flowers. Hard pruning includes either coppicing or cutting back to the bases of branches; new growth will be made from dormant buds in either case.

EVERGREEN TREES

Evergreens may fit either Group 1 or Group 2 but most require little pruning apart from 'tidying up' – unless parts suffer from winter cold damage. This will require minor trimming to remove damaged areas, mainly by cutting back to suitable side branches.

DEAD-HEADING

This involves removing old faded blooms, which diverts the plant's energy into new growth.

To remove, hold the flower between the thumb and first two fingers just above the dormant buds in the leaf axils and snap it off. Don't worry if the leaf and bud come away with the flower as there will be several others remaining.

Hold the faded flower gently and snap it off.

Shaping a hedge

A good shape for a hedge is a narrow A-shape, wider at the bottom than the top. This is more stable than a parallel-sided hedge and allows light to fall on the lower foliage. Use a frame to mark out the shape and then cut to that template when creating a hedge.

Many established hedges have an inverted A- or V-shape, and thus lose the lower foliage. Cutting with the shears pointing downwards often causes this. Always clip with the shears pointing upwards.

The right time for clipping varies with the species used and also with the purpose of the hedge. Conifer and broadleaved hedges should only need clipping once in late summer. Faster-growing hedging plants will need more frequent trimming. Broadleaved evergreens can be clipped just before they come into growth in the spring or at the end of summer. Informal hedges will need much less attention.

Pruning for foliage
A number of trees can be pruned to produce exotic foliage. These are mainly large-leafed ones, where vigorous regrowth can result in enormous leaves. The technique can also be used on plants with vividly coloured new foliage too.

PESTS AND DISEASES

This section details some of the most common pests and diseases that affect trees and provides information on how to combat them.

Anthracnose Caused by fungi that kill new leaves and shoots. They are more prevalent in cold wet summers, but generally new growth is made that is unaffected so the plant recovers. Anthracnose can also cause cankers. Remove all affected parts, burn them then spray the tree with benomyl or a copper-based fungicide.

Aphids Sap-sucking insects that can cause the death of shoot tips when present in large numbers, but the honeydew they secrete is more of a problem. Spray with a contact insecticide that only kills aphids, leaving their predators to mop up those missed by the spray.

Cankers These are lesions that appear on the stem or bark that are caused by a fungus or bacterium. The best solution is to remove the affected branch.

Coral spot Identified by pink rounded pustules on bark. The fungus can kill healthy tissue but is normally associated with stressed, dying or dead branches. Remove affected shoots and attend to any stress, ensuring water levels are satisfactory.

Fireblight A bacterial disease – infection is usually via flowers or new leaves. Remove affected shoots at least 60cm (2ft) below any signs of the disease, sterilising the blade between each cut.

Honey fungus A group of fungi that can be identified by the white mat of mycelium produced between the bark and wood. Resin may exude from the bark just above ground level. The best control is removal of dead roots, but is seldom practical. A phenol-based product is sold as a control measure.

Mildew Can cause serious harm to soft young foliage and in bad cases kills. The fungi form a white powdery covering and do not need damp conditions. Control is possible at an early stage by spraying with a fungicide.

Phytophthora A group of single-celled or yeast-like fungi that are spread through water. Phytophthora root disease kills the roots of many trees, causing sudden death. Remove and burn affected plants then improve soil drainage.

Scale insects Sap-sucking insects. Not a serious problem, but eradicate by washing stems with a soapy solution.

Silver leaf This fungal disease causes a brown discoloration of the current season's wood and, often, the foliage on the affected branch takes on a leadened or silver sheen. In mild cases, prune out affected branches or see if they recover naturally. In severe cases, remove the plant.

Wilt Causes the death of foliage and shoots by blocking the water conduction system. Examples of wilt are Dutch elm disease and verticillium wilt. Shows as a staining of the outer wood ring. Control by removing affected branches, sterilising the blade after each cut.

A–Z DIRECTORY OF PLANTS

This plant directory showcases the most commonly available garden trees. Listed alphabetically by Latin name these cover broadleaved woody plants, tall conifers and even bamboos, tree ferns and palms to provide planting ideas for many different styles of gardening and uses. These pages will inspire you as you create your own garden, and give you the practical know-how to look after each tree.

ABIES

Silver fir

Silver firs are so-named due to the silvery-white bands on the underside of the needles. They are evergreen conifers with regular whorls of branches and, usually, soft foliage. The female or seed cones are carried erect on the top side of the upper branches and can range in colour from violet purple through to green and brown. The male cones hang down from the lower branches and are designed to catch the wind and take the pollen onto nearby trees.

Abies koreana

In the garden, silver firs fit into a number of roles. *A. fraseri* and *A. koreana* are small trees with colourful cones and silvery foliage; they make excellent specimen plants for a lawn where there is not much space. *A. grandis* is a fast-growing large tree that makes a good specimen for a large garden or where it can be seen at the end of a vista.

All silver firs make good Christmas trees, with *A. nordmanniana* probably the best of all. Their immense advantage is that they drop few or no needles. They are best propagated from seed, sown in spring.

KEY FACTS
Soil Well-drained, moderately fertile to fertile, including chalk soils (except *A. procera*, which needs acidic soil)
Site Sun to moderate shade
Height 5m (16½ft); large varieties 7m (23ft)
Spread 3m (10ft)
Interest All varieties make good Christmas trees and produce fir cones. Some are fast-growing, others slow

CARE: Silver firs more or less look after themselves, and no special pruning is required. Aphids can cause some problems to these firs; also honey fungus is troublesome and can kill young trees.

ACACIA

Wattle

The wattles characterise the savannahs of East Africa and are also a major component of the forests of Australia. The hardy species of wattle, which can be used in gardens, originate from the areas in Australia.

The flowers are mainly yellow and carried over the winter/spring period. The species shown here have flowers in globular heads, but others have them in cylindrical 'bottle-brushes'. Although they are members of the legume family, they do not have the typical pea-like flowers; instead, the main attraction is the massed stamens.

The foliage of *Acacia* is also interesting. The standard foliage is bi-pinnate, with masses of small leaflets. However, this form only persists in species from moist environments. In drier climates, leaves are soon abandoned in favour of modified leaf stalks.

Acacia retinodes

Wattles are mainly trees or large shrubs for open sites in full sun. They are not reliably hardy, even in mild areas, so choose a sheltered site or grow them against a wall.

Acacia dealbata

KEY FACTS

Soil Plant in any suitable well-drained soil but avoid limey conditions

Site Plant in sun with side shelter away from any cold winds

Height Small varieties grow to 3m (10ft); others 10m (33ft)

Spread Small varieties 1.2m (4ft); others 8m (25ft)

Interest Yellow flowers in winter/spring and bi-pinnate foliage

CARE: Not much pruning required, except to remove any unsightly dieback. Fast-growing but half-hardy to frost tender. Relatively trouble-free; pests and diseases do not usually cause any particular problems.

ACER

Maple

The maples are a large genus of over 100 species and many cultivars. The species range greatly in size; most are deciduous, although there are some evergreens. Maples offer a range of attractive features, particularly with their foliage.

Foliage can vary from boldly lobed leaves to the delicately cut or dissected leaves of some selections of Japanese maple. The colour of the foliage is golden green in a number of selections, such as _Acer shirasawanum_ 'Aureum', purple in many forms of _A. palmatum_ and _A. platanoides_ and various hues of green in others. In autumn, the colours can be spectacular. Flowers are not their strongest feature. By contrast, the bark of maples can be the most striking feature, such as with the various snake-bark maples (see p. 33).

Maples divide into those that are naturally under-storey trees, and those that are large, dominant forest trees.

Acer shirasawanum 'Aureum'

Japanese maples

These are mainly cultivars of *A. palmatum* but also include two other Japanese species (*A. japonicum* and *A. shirasawanum*) and the closely related *A. circinatum* (vine maple) from western North America. They make large shrubs, reaching about 4m (13ft) in 10 years, but will grow on to make trees 6–15m (20–50ft) in 50–100 years. They tolerate light to moderate shade and also like protection from spring frosts and cold dry winds; in the garden use hardy screening plants, such as bamboos or other shrubs, to provide shelter.

Japanese maples are the structural plants of most Japanese-style gardens, and are very effective if planted to reflect over water. They can also make useful plants for containers. Care with watering is important, otherwise the foliage will become brown between the veins. Vine weevil can be a bugbear to maples in containers.

Acer palmatum 'Garnet'

Snake-bark maples

Snake-bark maples belong to a distinct section in the genus that includes about 20 species. Their chief horticultural character is in the bark. This is green (or red in one-year shoots and candy-pink in *Acer pensylvanicum* 'Erythrocladum') and fissures to reveal pure white striations running up and down the trunk like a snake. The bark feature is present throughout the year, but is at its best for the winter season. It is shown off to best effect in vigorously growing trees.

Snake-bark maples attain 6–8m (20–25ft) in about 15 years but grow very slowly thereafter. They make great specimen trees. The habit is arching, with weeping outer branchlets. When planting into lawns, keep a good 1m (3ft) radius clear of grass, as the bark is easily damaged by mowers.

Acer davidii

Small maple trees

Small tree maples offer a number of characteristics, and can eventually grow to around 8–12m (25–40ft). The paperbark maple, *Acer griseum*, has cinnamon-coloured bark that peels off in thin, paper-like flakes, looking attractive throughout the year. It also has excellent autumn colour; red and scarlet. It grows best in well-drained acidic loams. Another species with trifoliate leaves is *Acer maximowicziana* (syn. *Acer nikkoense*). In autumn the foliage colours to orange and red. In *Acer cappadocicum* 'Aureum', the leaves soon become golden yellow.

Acer griseum

Large maple trees

These larger trees are bold specimen trees, rather too big for the average garden but well suited to distant parts of larger gardens. They have the potential to reach around 20m (65ft) high with domed crowns 20m (65ft) across. *Acer platanoides*, the Norway maple, is one of the few maples worth planting for the flowers – these are pale yellow and open just before the leaves. In purple-leafed forms the flowers are tinged with red.

The sycamore, *Acer pseudoplatanus*, is a pet hate of many gardeners, due to its ability to seed freely.

However, provided their heads are chopped off at the stage when only the pair of cotyledons show, they are easily controlled. When mature, a tree sycamore can be absolutely majestic.

KEY FACTS

Soil Any well-drained soil – preferably fertile and deep if it is chalky

Site Sun or light shade

Height Small varieties 2.5m (8m); large varieties 9m (30ft)

Spread Small varieties 2.5m (8m); large varieties 6m (20ft)

Interest Attractive foliage; many species have great autumn colour too. Some species have striking bark

Acer pseudoplatanus 'Brilliantissimum'

CARE: Maples tend to bleed if cut; this is reduced if they are pruned in midsummer. Mulch the soil to aid moisture retention in the summer, and also to control weeds. Verticillium wilt and coral spot can affect many species. Tar spot and aphids can affect leaves but do little harm.

AESCULUS   *Horse chestnut or Buckeye*

Horse chestnut (*Aesculus hippocastanum*) is widely grown for the large candles of white flowers with pink, red or yellow spots that rise from buds on last year's shoots in mid- to late spring – as well as for its conkers. It grows at a steady 30–40cm (12–16in) a year until 20m (70ft) in height, by which time it is a large tree with a high domed crown.

The cultivar 'Baumannii' is sterile, setting no seed. It is useful for sites where it is unsafe for children to hurl sticks to get the conkers down. But if you have space for *Aesculus hippocastanum* in your garden, plant the fertile form. The red horse chestnut (*Aesculus carnea*) has rose-pink flowers.

There are other species to choose from. *Aesculus neglecta* 'Erythroblastos' is a small tree whose new foliage is a brilliant shrimp pink, slowly fading to yellow-green. As a spring foliage plant, it is outstanding. *Aesculus parviflora* is a suckering shrub and no garden is too small for it. However, the best species is the medium-sized Indian horse chestnut, *Aesculus indica*. The flowers are some six weeks later than the horse chestnut. The only thing to be aware with this species is that it can be damaged by spring frost when it is young.

KEY FACTS

Soil Will grow well in any good, moist but well-drained garden soil, including chalk

Site Grow in sun or partial shade

Height *A. parviflora* 2m (6½ft); others, up to 7m (23ft)

Spread *A. parviflora* 3m (10ft); others, up to 7m (23ft)

Interest Grown for its flowers and conkers. A great large tree for big gardens, although there are smaller species to choose from too

Aesculus indica

CARE: No pruning needed, except to maintain a good shape or thin out the dense foliage. Apply mulch to retain moisture in the soil during the summer and prevent early leaf-fall. A leaf blotch can cause unsightly foliage and early leaf loss; also prone to canker, coral spot and scale insects.

AILANTHUS

Tree of Heaven

Ailanthus altissima, the most interesting and commonly cultivated species, produces summer flowers that are greenish white. The female trees produce the seeds; immature fruits are red or green. The foliage is red coloured in spring and is normally 30–60cm (1–2ft) long. However, on vigorous young trees it can be 1m (3ft). The autumn colour is negligible, although the bark is fissured with buff streaks. *Ailanthus* makes a vigorous specimen tree, ideal for a large garden, probably making 15m (50ft) in 20–25 years.

KEY FACTS

Soil Any; avoid waterlogged sites
Site Sun or partial shade
Height 15m (50ft) in 20–25 years; ultimate size can reach 25m (80ft)
Spread Eventually reaches 15m (50ft)
Interest Grown for its foliage and winged fruit

Ailanthus altissima

CARE: No pruning needed except to restrict size – coppice in late winter. Watch out for suckers growing in the wrong places; manure and mulch for best foliage. Trouble-free.

ALNUS

Alder

Alders are often found growing beside water, especially the native common alder, *Alnus glutinosa*. However, they will thrive in any normal garden soil except shallow chalky ones, and are able to tolerate the poor conditions found in swampy sites.

Alders are at home in the water garden but are useful in a number of other locations. Their chief horticultural merit is in the male catkins. These expand in late winter or early spring, giving a purple (*Alnus glutinosa*), red (*Alnus incana*) or yellow (*Alnus cordata*) haze to the tree. The woody cones follow and can be used for festive decorations or in flower arrangements. The autumn colour is usually poor. The forms of grey alder, *Alnus incana*, include the 'Aurea' with yellow green foliage, and the weeping 'Pendula'.

Alders are used for shelter plantings in orchards as they come into leaf and flower earlier than apples

CARE: Prune to restrict size once the leaves have fallen in the autumn. Fully hardy and tolerant of a variety of conditions so very little maintenance generally needed. A water-borne phytophthora species is causing problems on common alder grown beside rivers.

Alnus

and other fruit trees, therefore giving protection against spring frosts. They are also small trees that do not spread widely.

KEY FACTS

Soil Wet to well-drained, acidic to neutral soils. *A. incana* is tolerant of drier sites and chalk soils

Site Plant in a sunny position; excellent near water but this is not an essential requirement

Height *A. incana* 6m (20ft); others 10m (33ft)

Spread *A. incana* 3m (10ft); others 6m (20ft)

Interest Produces colourful catkins and woody cones

Alnus incana

AMELANCHIER

Snowy mespilus

These are deciduous shrubs or small shrubby trees. They are grown mainly for the snowy white flowers in late spring that emerge with, or just ahead of, the foliage. The new foliage is a coppery red for a few days. The fruits ripen in early to midsummer but are normally quickly eaten by birds. They are black or purplish red and like miniature apples. Autumn colour – red and orange – is excellent too.

Snowy mespilus make excellent large shrubs for a border, as a backcloth or boundary planting, or as a specimen tree in the lawn.

Amelanchier lamarckii

KEY FACTS

Soil Well-drained to moist and acidic to neutral; avoid chalk soils
Site Sun to moderate shade
Height 2.5m (8ft)
Spread 2.5m (8ft)
Interest Grown for its white flowers; also produces fruit

CARE: Prune only to restrict the size. Very easy to grow but can suffer from fireblight.

ARALIA

Devil's walking stick or Japanese angelica tree

This tree is so-named because of the suckers it throws. These do not branch until they are 2m (6ft) high. Instead, they appear as stout rods or walking sticks that are covered in dense, sharp spines. The foliage consists of huge compound leaves, which are bi-pinnate and rather deltoid. The flowers are white and appear in autumn. *Aralia* should be planted in a shrub bed or as a specimen small tree.

Aralia elata

KEY FACTS

Soil Needs well-drained to moist soil
Site This plant likes sun or dappled shade
Height 5m (16½ft)
Spread 3m (10ft)
Interest Its bold foliage

CARE: Prune to restrict size or coppice for bold foliage. On too fertile sites, the wood is pithy and liable to frost damage over winter. Fairly trouble-free from pests and diseases.

ARAUCARIA

Monkey puzzle

The common name refers to the viciously sharp foliage, which makes climbing these trees tricky. *Araucaria araucana* is a medium-sized evergreen tree with an open, whorled crown. At its best, the foliage descends to ground level, setting off the trunk – which is grey and wrinkled like an elephant's hide. The fruits are on large rounded cones, which are carried at the tips of the branches on female trees. In the garden the tree is excellent as a specimen planting, but does need space. It is less happy in small front gardens, but is very tolerant of coastal exposure.

KEY FACTS

Soil Well-drained, acidic or alkaline
Site Full sun
Height 2.5m (8ft)
Spread 2m (6½ft)
Interest Slow- but steady-growing, excellent as a specimen

Araucaria araucana

CARE: No pruning required. Honey fungus can be a problem.

ARBUTUS

Strawberry tree or Madroñe

These evergreen trees and large shrubs are members of the heather family. *Arbutus unedo* is the best for flowers and fruits. The white blooms are carried in the autumn at the same time that the fruits from last year ripen. Two other species produce outstanding bark – smooth and peeling in large sheets – *Arbutus menziesii* and *A. andrachnoides*.

Arbutus menziesii can make a large tree, albeit slow-growing, whereas the other two are shrub trees. They should be used as focal points.

KEY FACTS
Soil Prefers well-drained soils but tolerates chalk, lime and acid sands
Site Grows best in sun to light shade
Height 2.5m (8ft)
Spread 2.5m (8ft)
Interest Flowers and fruit. Two species produce impressive bark

Arbutus unedo

CARE: No pruning required. *A. unedo* will coppice if it needs reshaping. Shelter the species when young. A fungus can cause blotches on the leaves but leaves no real damage.

BETULA

Birch

Betula

The birches include some of the most 'garden worthy' of small trees. The male catkins in spring provide an attractive display before the leaves emerge, but other assets include their bark, foliage, habit and spectacular autumn colour. In many birches, the bark is rich in betulin, a compound that gives it a vivid whiteness. Birches will make trees 10–15m (33–50ft) in height over 20–30 years. They are surface rooting and will compete for soil moisture.

KEY FACTS

Soil Freely drained soil
Site Prefers sunny sites
Height *B. pendula* 5m (16½ft); others 8m (25ft)
Spread *B. pendula* 2m (6½ft); others 5m (16½ft)
Interest Attractive catkins, bark, foliage, habit and autumn colour

Betula jacquemontii

CARE: Minimal pruning needed. Avoid cutting in late winter/early spring as they will bleed. No major problems: moribund and recently dead trees host the birch polypore bracket fungus (*P. betulinus*).

BUDDLEJA

Butterfly bush

These are chiefly grown for the very colourful and fragrant flowers, which have a strong honey scent and whose nectar attracts butterflies. The principal species in cultivation is *Buddleja davidii*.

The attraction of *Buddleja* is that they provide fast-growing, medium shrubs or small trees that require very little maintenance. Left to its own devices, *Buddleja davidii* makes a small semi-evergreen tree perhaps 6m (20ft) in height and 4m (13ft) across. Having reached this size it virtually stops growing.

Buddleja davidii 'Pink Delight'

KEY FACTS

Soil Most soils as long as they are well-drained
Site Plant these in a hot sunny position in the garden
Height 3m (10ft)
Spread 3m (10ft)
Interest Colourful flowers that attract butterflies

CARE: All species can be coppiced and pruned, but make sure you know when your particular *Buddleja* flowers, so that you can prune accordingly. Usually trouble-free.

BUXUS

Box

Box has small, evergreen leaves and much smaller, insignificant flowers. It is valuable in the garden because it is very tolerant of clipping. This makes it one of the best shrubs to use for topiaries and living sculptures. It is also excellent for hedges. The wild or normal form of the species can make a narrow crowned tree over time, able to make 10m (33ft) but more often a rounded bush to 6m (20ft).

KEY FACTS

Soil Well-drained soil; this plant has a slight preference for alkaline soils
Site Moderate sun to shade
Height 2m (6½ft)
Spread 2m (6½ft)
Interest Evergreen; great as topiary or a hedge

Buxus sempervirens

CARE: No pruning necessary, but species tolerates it wonderfully. Full sun and strong winds can lead to foliage scorch, otherwise it is relatively trouble-free.

CALOCEDRUS

Incense cedar

The incense cedar makes a tight, columnar, evergreen tree in cultivation. It has flat sprays of foliage that are glossy and dark green in colour. In some ways it resembles the narrow-crowned forms of Lawson cypress (*see* pp 56–7) but it has two distinct advantages over these: it is not susceptible to either honey fungus or phytophthora root rot, which makes it an excellent choice for places where such diseases have been a problem.

KEY FACTS

Soil Well-drained soil, acidic or alkaline; even sands or chalk

Site Full sun

Height 3m (10ft)

Spread 1m (3ft)

Interest Good evergreen tree for a tight space due to its narrow, upright habit

Calocedrus decurrens

CARE: No pruning required but it can be clipped. It is also fairly trouble-free from pests and diseases.

CARPINUS

Hornbeam

The name hornbeam is Anglo-Saxon in origin, with horn being 'hard' and beam meaning 'tree'. The timber is indeed very tough and is often used for chopping boards. In the garden, hornbeams are used either as specimen trees for the neat foliage, smooth silvery grey bark and attractive autumn colour or for hedging. Although deciduous, the leaves on juvenile plants are retained over winter to give the plant winter protection, and regular clipping keeps it in the juvenile phase. The male catkins are yellow and open in advance of the leaves.

Carpinus betulus

KEY FACTS

Soil Heavy clays to light gravels
Site This plant prefers sun to moderate shade
Height 5m (16½ft)
Spread 4m (13ft)
Interest Good as a specimen, due to its neat foliage, silvery bark and good autumn colour, or as hedging

CARE: Avoid pruning in spring as they will bleed. Trim hedges in summer. Generally trouble-free.

CASTANEA

Sweet chestnut or
Spanish chestnut

This genus is related to the oaks. It is cultivated in temperate regions for the tasty fruit – chestnuts. The midsummer flowers are quite showy and formed at the end of the current season's shoots. They consist of a spike of whitish-yellow male flowers with the female flowers at the base. The fruits ripen in the autumn to a burr of vicious spines that protect the nuts.

Castanea sativa

Castanea is adapted to hot dry summers. In the garden, it is useful as a specimen tree and as a coppice tree.

KEY FACTS
Soil Well-drained; dry, acidic sand
Site Sun to moderate shade
Height 7m (23ft)
Spread 5m (16½ft)
Interest Grown for its edible chestnuts and showy flowers

CARE: No pruning necessary. Coppice on a 10–15 year cycle for firewood or poles. *Castanea* can be troubled by phytophthora root disease and chestnut blight.

CATALPA

Bean tree

Bean trees have large erect panicles that are carried in mid- to late summer. The bell-shaped flowers are usually white with spots of red, yellow and purple, and are often fragrant. The fruits are long slender pods that open to release the small two-winged seeds. *Catalpa* have large, heart-shaped leaves. These are ideal trees for large gardens. They can be coppiced; well-manured specimens will produce enormous foliage.

KEY FACTS

Soil Well-drained, moisture-retentive soils
Site Full sun and shelter
Height 5m (16½ft)
Spread 5m (16½ft)
Interest Produces long, slender fruit pods and fragrant, bell-shaped flowers

Catalpa bignonioides

CARE: No pruning regime required except to restrict or reshape the tree. Can be coppiced. It is late leafing but can be frost tender when young. Verticillium wilt can kill or damage it so keep a careful lookout for this starting.

CEDRUS

Cedar

The cedars are some of the most stately of evergreen trees originating from areas in the western Himalayas and the Mediterranean. With their large, spreading branches, cedars are extremely majestic-looking trees. Because of the potential size of some species, make sure you have a garden that can provide ample space before buying – otherwise they won't be able to reach their full growth potential.

Your timespan and available space should dictate which species to choose. *Cedrus deodara* is the most attractive as a small tree, until it is about 10m (33ft) in height. For a small garden, it is the best species and should be chopped down and replaced every 15–20 years. *C. atlantica* looks beautiful from age 10 onwards. It is ideal for moderate spaces. *C. libani* is wonderful from around 100 years – assuming you can wait that long! – by which time it has developed its level branching habit.

Cedars can be raised from seed sown in spring or by grafting onto seedling rootstocks. The male cones emerge above the branches in autumn and the female cones expand during the next summer and ripen in late summer, falling apart sometime over the winter/spring period.

KEY FACTS

Soil These cedars will grow on any well-drained soil, including chalk and acidic sands

Site As much sun as possible – these plants abhor shade

Height 4.5m (14³⁄₄ft)

Spread 3m (10ft)

Interest Evergreen, majestic specimen trees that produce cones

CARE: No pruning required, but, if trimming, always leave live foliage on a branch or it will die. Grafted plants may benefit from being trained up to form a straight leader. The various cedars can all be susceptible to honey fungus; also some species of aphids can cause them problems.

Cedrus atlantica (male cones)

CERCIDIPHYLLUM

Katsura tree

This tree, originating from China and Japan, is grown for the rounded, heart-shaped leaves, attractive habit and, most of all, for its brilliant autumn colour. The latter is a mixture of yellows, scarlets, crimsons, pinks and golds. The new foliage, however, is usually bronzed. The flowers are insignificant and the small green pod-like fruits are only carried on female trees. *Cercidiphyllum* makes a very good specimen tree.

KEY FACTS

Soil Humus-rich, moisture-retentive soil
Site Sun to light shade
Height 7m (23ft)
Spread 4m (13ft)
Interest Great autumn colour and attractive habit

Cercidiphyllum japonicum

CARE: No pruning required, except for restricting or reshaping. Shelter from spring frosts if possible. This tree is not usually affected by pests and diseases.

CERCIS

Judas tree

Cercis has pink or white pea-like flowers that are carried on the older branches, often directly on the trunk. The flowers are followed by the typical legume pod, showing it as a member of this family, but it is almost unique in having simple heart-shaped leaves. It has no reliable autumn colour but sometimes turns a clear yellow. A slow-growing tree, it will slowly make 8–12m (25–39ft) over 30 years or so. It is best used as a specimen tree in a lawn area. *Cercis* tolerates acid sands and chalky soils but will not stand waterlogged or very heavy soils.

KEY FACTS

Soil Any well-drained soil
Site Sun or light shade
Height 6m (20ft)
Spread 4m (13ft)
Interest Slow-growing, flowering specimen tree with heart-shaped leaves

Cercis canadensis 'Forest Pansy'

CARE: No pruning required, except for restricting or reshaping. Mulch to keep the soil moist in summer. Verticillium wilt and coral spot can cause problems.

CHAMAECYPARIS
Cypress

Chamaecyparis, literally false cypress, is a small, evergreen genus but one that has had a major impact upon horticulture. The main species is Lawson cypress, *Chamaecyparis lawsoniana*, from northwest America. This has produced hundreds of different forms, many of which are dwarf or slow-growing. The tree forms range from the golden yellow foliage of 'Stewartii' to the narrow habit of 'Columnaris' with pale, blue-grey foliage.

In the garden, Lawson cypress makes an excellent specimen tree with its narrow habit and dense foliage. Older trees tend to lose the tight habit and develop crowns with some short spreading branches with pendulous tips. Lawson cypress makes excellent hedges. Like most other conifers, it can only be clipped into live foliage but the growth rate is not too fast. Unpruned trees can also be used for screening.

KEY FACTS
Soil Any well-drained soil, both acidic and alkaline
Site Sun or a light shade
Height 3m (10ft)
Spread 1.2m (4ft)
Interest Excellent specimen tree or hedge, this is a slow-growing conifer

Chamaecyparis lawsoniana 'Columnaris'

CARE: Can be clipped provided there is live (green) foliage left on the shoot. Avoid depressions where water may sit, as trees in these sites are liable to phytophthora root rot. Honey fungus can also kill trees.

Cladrastis

CLADRASTIS
Yellow wood

The Latin name *Cladrastis* translates as 'yellow wood' and this tree is a member of the legume family. *Cladrastis kentukea* has fragrant white flowers that are carried in enormous pendent clusters, but these are only produced following a hot, dry summer and are rare in gardens. It has pinnate foliage and a yellow-orange autumnal colour. *Cladrastis sinensis* produces bluish-white, fragrant flowers very freely and is a worthy summer-flowering tree. Both species make excellent specimen trees and will thrive on a wide range of well-drained soils, especially friable loams.

Cladrastis kentukea

KEY FACTS
Soil Well-drained loams
Site Sun to light shade
Height 6m (20ft)
Spread 5m (16½ft)
Interest Grown for the pea-like flowers and autumn foliage

CARE: Avoid pruning in winter/spring as it will bleed. The branches are brittle so liable to fracture in strong winds. Fairly trouble-free, but can suffer from verticillium wilt.

CORNUS

Cornel or Dogwood

This is a large group of plants. Botanically they are several, albeit-related, genera but in horticultural terms they are generally all listed as *Cornus*. The species here are best considered as belonging to three genera: *Cornus* in the narrow sense, in which the flowers are in dense umbels enclosed by two or more bracts and which appear before the leaves (i.e. *Cornus mas*); Swida, with the flowers in large heads without bracts (including *Cornus alternifolia* and *Cornus controversa*) and Benthamidia, with the clusters of small flowers subtended by four (or six) large white or reddish bracts. All three species have variegated forms.

Cornels are useful in the garden. *Cornus mas* is one of the earliest woody harbingers of spring, opening its yellow flowers in late winter. Where they excel is in the tiered foliage – flat or slightly

Cornus kousa var. *chinensis*

drooping plates of foliage on which the flower clusters are supported above the leaves. They are worth planting for this architectural form alone. There are species that are suited to smaller spaces, making multi-stemmed shrubs, and others that are good specimen trees when they are planted in a lawn setting.

Cornus kousa var. *chinensis* 'Satomi'

The large-flowered *Cornus* are showy for the bracts, which form a plate below the cluster of totally inconspicuous flowers. There are usually four bracts, but *Cornus nuttallii* often has six. The bracts cover the flowers in bud, slowly expanding in spring. At its best, the branches can be wreathed in flowers and the leaves almost entirely hidden. *Cornus kousa*, especially the var. *chinensis*, forms a broad conical large shrub to small tree, making 8–10m (25–33ft) after 20 to 30 years. It is the most reliable of this group, tolerating most garden soils including chalky ones provided they are not too shallow.

Cornus florida is a smaller shrub, attaining only 4–5m (13–16½ft) in the average garden. It can be stunning in full bloom but never quite lives up to the quality when wild in its native eastern North America. *C. nuttallii* makes a tall tree, 15–25m (50–80ft) when wild in its native western North America, but more usually 8–12m (25–39ft) in cultivation.

Cornus 'Eddie's White Wonder' is a hybrid of *C. florida* and *C. nuttallii*. It will make a large shrub or small tree and is spectacular in spring. *Cornus* 'Norman Haddon' is a hybrid of *Cornus kousa* with *Cornus capitata* (an evergreen, yellow-flowered species).

KEY FACTS

Soil Likes well-drained soils, including chalky soils (except *C. florida*)
Site Sun to light shade
Height 7m (23ft)
Spread 4m (13ft)
Interest Tiered foliage and architectural form. All flower and some species also produce fruit

Cornus florida 'Rainbow'

CARE: No particular pruning requirements, except for restricting or reshaping. Fairly straightforward to cultivate and maintain – mulch to keep soil moist during the summer. Relatively trouble-free.

CORYLUS *Hazel*

Corylus includes the native hazel or cobnut (*Corylus avellana*), which is a major under-storey tree in forests and forest margins. This is one of the species that provides hazelnuts, the other being the filbert, *Corylus maxima*.

All the hazels are valuable for their showy male catkins. These open sometime in late winter, lasting into early spring. The colour of the catkins ranges from lemon-yellow to a more browny yellow. The female flowers are modest, comprising only 12–15 crimson stigmas of which only 1–2mm (less than $^1/_{10}$in) poke out from a green bud.

Corylus avellana 'Contorta' is a form with twisted branches. It is a genetic oddity that has lost the ability to grow shoots in a straight line. It can look good in the winter tracery of the branches, especially when laden with pendent catkins. *Corylus maxima* 'Purpurea' is a purple-leafed form, with the catkins also purple. It is particularly useful as a backcloth for plants with light golden foliage.

C. avellana and *C. maxima* are multi-stemmed shrubs, while the Turkish hazel, *Corylus colurna*, is a tree with a single straight bole, making 15m (50ft) in a garden setting. It is attractive in catkin but it also has very interesting bark – ash-grey or buff brown that flakes in thin scaly flecks too.

KEY FACTS

Soil *Corylus* is suitable for any type of soil except waterlogged ones – from acidic to alkaline

Site The plant prefers a sunny site through to moderate shade

Height 7m (23ft)

Spread 6m (20ft)

Interest Showy male catkins. The fruiting forms also provide excellent edible nuts

Corylus avellana 'Contorta'

CARE: Will coppice readily; best when stems are replaced every five or so years. *Corylus* is easy to manage. A variety of insects and mites affect these trees, but not seriously enough to cause lasting damage.

COTINUS

Smoke tree

The common name for this plant is derived from the way in which it is smothered by the flowers from early summer onwards. These are expanded panicles that contain many sterile flowers, each with long, thread-like plumose stalks. The stalks persist as summer turns into autumn and the flowers into far fewer fruits.

Cotinus **'Grace'**

However, it makes them worth their spot in the shrub border or as a specimen at the edge of a sea of grass. Most of the forms in cultivation have purple foliage, and in these the flower stalks have a purplish tinge. In the natural green form the stalks start a shade of fawn and end as smoky-grey. The autumn colour is even better, normally a strong, vivid red but in some forms orange-red.

Cotinus coggygria will thrive on chalk but the American species, *Cotinus obovatus*, requires a neutral or acidic soil.

KEY FACTS

Soil Any well-drained soil – an unfussy plant

Site Enjoys a position with lots of sun

Height 5m (16½ft)

Spread 5m (16½ft)

Interest Smothered in flowers from early summer. Great autumn colour too

CARE: Only prune to remove damage or to shorten wayward stems. Avoid over-fertile sites, which can result in a proliferation of foliage, no flowers and less autumn colour. Powdery mildew can be a problem on purple forms; verticillium wilt occasionally kills branches.

COTONEASTER

The cotoneasters considered here are the taller-growing forms, which can make large shrubs or small trees. These forms all have masses of white flowers, which, while individually small, produce quite a display – and makes them attractive to bees. They have lots of uses in the garden, apart from the obvious colour of their flowers and fruits. As berrying plants, they provide winter food for many birds. When the individual fruit is eaten depends upon a number of factors. Location is an important consideration – if the bush is close to shelter where birds can feel

Cotoneaster salicifolius

secure, it tends to be stripped much sooner than if it is in an exposed position.

Some species ripen much later than others. It is possible to manipulate the choice of species and siting so that natural bird food is available for much of the winter. The red-fruited forms, such as 'Cornubia' and 'John Waterer', tend to be eaten more quickly than the yellow-fruited forms 'Exburyensis' and 'Rothschildianus'.

The larger cotoneasters are also useful in the shrub bed as evergreen screens, as small specimen trees and as effective hedging. *Cotoneaster lacteus* is excellent both as a screen and as a wall shrub.

KEY FACTS

Soil Any well-drained soil is fine
Site Prefers sun to moderate shade
Height 6m (20ft)
Spread 5m (16½ft)
Interest Evergreens that produce colourful flowers and fruit. Good shrubs or small specimen trees; can be used as screening or hedging

CARE: No pruning regime is necessary, but they can be trimmed to keep to size. The only care needed is to mulch and feed to keep vigorous. Cotoneasters are members of the apple subfamily so prone to fireblight. Also honey fungus, silver leaf and various insects can affect them.

CRATAEGUS

May or hawthorn

May (*Crataegus monogyna*), especially the wild white form, is one of the most attractive of all small flowering trees. It makes a domed crown with pendent branches that are wreathed with small clusters of scented white flowers, followed by maroon-red fruits in autumn. The forms of *Crataegus laevigata* with pink or scarlet flowers have a similar habit. Other species include *C. lavallei* 'Carrierei' and *Crataegus persimilis* 'Prunifolia'. These small trees are useful as specimens. They also make excellent hedges, tolerating clipping.

KEY FACTS

Soil Any heavy to well-drained soil, including chalk
Site Sun to moderate shade
Height 5m (16½ft)
Spread 6m (20ft)
Interest Small flowering tree; excellent as hedging

Crataegus laevigata 'Rosea Flore Pleno'

CARE: Very tolerant of clipping but no specific pruning regime needed. Beware the thorns. Can suffer from insect and fungal problems but generally not adversely affected.

CRYPTOMERIA

Japanese cedar

Cryptomeria japonica makes a vigorous, evergreen, upright tree with a columnar-conic habit. It is one of the few conifers that will coppice if cut down. *Cryptomeria* has given rise to a large number of forms, including many dwarfs. 'Sekkan-sugi', with creamy-yellow foliage that turns white in winter, is one of the most effective cultivars. There is a stabilised juvenile form, forma *elegans*, with long soft foliage, which will breed true. In the garden, use the tree form as a specimen tree, with ornate cultivars like 'Sekkan-sugi' and *elegans* as shrubs for smaller spaces.

KEY FACTS

Soil Well-drained but moist
Site Sun to light shade
Height dwarfs 2.5m (8ft); others 4m (13ft)
Spread dwarfs 1.2m (4ft); others 2m (6½ft)
Interest Evergreen conifer

Cryptomeria japonica f. *elegans*

CARE: Can be coppiced or simply pruned to be cut back. Relatively trouble-free and does not have major problems with pests and diseases.

CUNNINGHAMIA

China fir

The foliage is similar to the monkey puzzle tree (*see* p. 43), but not so sharp or hard. The genus coppices and trees are often surrounded by a cluster of suckers at the base of the trunk. At its best it makes a very attractive and interesting specimen tree. It likes a moist site with good ground water and, if allowed to dry out during the summer, the older foliage tends to turn brown and fall. It is perfectly hardy.

KEY FACTS

Soil Best when planted in well-drained, deep and fertile soil
Site This tree prefers sun to light shade
Height 3m (10ft)
Spread 1.2m (4ft)
Interest Coniferous, this makes a very attractive specimen tree

Cunninghamia lanceolata

CARE: The genus tolerates coppicing and clipping. Shelter from cold winds and keep the soil moist during dry periods. Relatively trouble-free – does not have major problems from pests and diseases.

CUPRESSUS

Cypress

Tolerance of drought and chalky soils characterise some of the true cypresses, especially *Cupressus glabra* (*C. arizonica* var. *glabra*). This makes a small to medium tree with a dense conical habit and blue-grey foliage. The reddish-purple and smooth bark peels to reveal pale patches beneath.

Like all the true cypresses, the cones take two years to ripen. *Cupressus sempervirens* is mainly grown as the narrow, crowned form so typical of the Mediterranean landscape. *C. macrocarpa* can make a large tree and looks very similar to a cedar of Lebanon when over 100 years old (although it is much faster-growing). The hardiest cypress is nootka cypress (*C. nootkatensis*). Leyland cypress is a hybrid between *C. macrocarpa* and *C. nootkatensis*. This cypress is

Cupressus macrocarpa 'Goldcrest'

usually referred to as *Cupressocyparis leylandii*.
Cypresses make good specimen evergreen trees.
They can all be grown from cuttings, most easily
if these are taken during the late summer.

KEY FACTS

Soil Well-drained, acidic to alkaline; can get chlorotic on shallow chalk soils

Site Much prefer a sunnier site – cypresses are not suitable for shady positions

Height Small varieties 3.5m (11½ft); others 8m (25ft)

Spread Narrow varieties 1m (3ft); others 2.5m (8ft)

Interest Coniferous; good evergreen specimen tree

Cypressus sempervirens 'Stricta

CARE: Will not regrow unless there is live (green) foliage, so do not clip into brown branches. When transplanting best grown in pots and plant out small as coarse root system does not establish freely. Corynium canker can weaken, even kill, entire trees; also affected by honey fungus and phytophthora root rot.

CYDONIA

Quince

This is the classical quince, which is the source of the original (Portuguese) marmalade. It makes a small deciduous tree that, in late spring, carries large, single white flowers. In autumn, the fruit follows. These are pear-shaped, ripening from green to light golden yellow, with lovely fragrant flesh. The bark is attractive in its own right, smooth and purplish-grey, and flakes to reveal orange beneath. In autumn, the foliage turns yellow. Quince should not be restricted to the orchard or, as is common, being rootstock for orchard pears. Rather, use it in the garden as a small specimen tree.

KEY FACTS

Soil Well-drained, acidic soil
Site Sun or dappled shade
Height 4m (13ft)
Spread 4m (13ft)
Interest Small deciduous specimen tree with attractive bark. Fragrant fruit follows the flowers

Cydonia oblonga

CARE: No pruning is necessary, except to restrict or reshape the tree. Be aware that the seeds are poisonous. Mulch when grown on light soils. Quince can suffer from the usual range of orchard apple bugs.

DAVIDIA

Dove tree

The large white bracts that make this tree special are in pairs, flopped over the cluster of male flowers containing only stamens with a single female flower near the tip. The bracts give the appearance of doves resting in the tree, hence the common name. The leaves are similar to those of the lime tree, turning yellow in the autumn. The fruit is a hard oblong green drupe (*see* p. 146) that hangs down from the boughs in autumn, usually persisting until spring.

KEY FACTS

Soil Heavy to well-drained, acidic or alkaline soils
Site Sun to light shade
Height 6m (20ft)
Spread 5m (16½ft)
Interest Spring-flowering tree; produces large white bracts and fruit in autumn

Davidia involucrata **var.** *vilmoriniana*

CARE: No special pruning regime is required. The tree takes a year or two to establish, mulch and water as needed. It does not seem to have any particular problems with pests and diseases.

DRIMYS

Winter's bark

This is an evergreen genus of 30 species of shrubs and trees that have handsome, aromatic leaves. They are usually grown for the fragrant ivory-white flowers that terminate the shoots in early summer.

The fruit of the *Drimys* is a fleshy carpel containing a number of seeds, and can also be used as a pepper substitute. Grow this genus in a sheltered position in lime-free soils.

KEY FACTS

Soil Prefers well-drained, moisture-retentive soil
Site Light shade
Height 4m (13ft)
Spread 3m (10ft)
Interest Fragrant summer flowers, aromatic leaves and fruit

Drimys winteri

CARE: If needed, prune after flowering (Group 1 – *see* p. 21). Plant in spring after risk of frosts is passed. Does not have any particular problems with pests and diseases.

ELAEAGNUS
Oleaster

This genus includes both deciduous and evergreen species. The evergreens have some rich leaf markings, with speckles of gold or white, while the deciduous species have silvery leaves. The flowers are not overtly showy but are fragrant. The fruits are an oblong drupe (*see* p. 146) with a single seed. The fleshy layer is sweet and juicy. All parts of the plants are covered with scales. Oleaster are good for coastal sites.

KEY FACTS
Soil Light/sandy, avoid rich soil
Site Sun for deciduous; sun/light shade for evergreens
Height 5m (16½ft)
Spread 5m (16½ft)
Interest Both deciduous and evergreen species have attractive leaves. Early summer- and autumn-flowering species

Elaeagnus ebbingei 'Limelight'

CARE: Prune only to reshape. Vigorous growths may need tying in. This genus does not have any particular problems with pests and diseases.

EMBOTHRIUM
Chilean fire bush

The tubular waxy flowers, which are scarlet and borne in axillary and terminal racemes in late spring, are reminiscent of fire. Despite its common name, however, the Chilean fire bush usually makes a narrow crowned tree rather than a bush.

It is one of the most flamboyant of evergreen spring-flowering trees when at its prime. Use it as an exclamation plant where it will be prominent when in leaf and flower. In colder or more exposed gardens, offer shelter but in milder locations it will flourish when planted in the open.

KEY FACTS
Soil Moisture-retentive, acidic/neutral soil
Site Sun to light woodland
Height 5m (16½ft)
Spread 2m (6½ft)
Interest Flamboyant spring flowers; evergreen tree

Embothrium coccineum

CARE: Prune after flowering if needed. Protect from cold drying winds. Does not have any particular problems with pests and diseases.

EUCALYPTUS

This genus contains about 600 or so species originating from Australia. Most are not hardy but quite a few are, leaving a large number from which to choose. Most of the hardy species, colloquially known as 'gums', have a bark that exfoliates, revealing white, green and yellow at different stages. The leaves are evergreen. In the adult phase they are identical on both sides and usually hang down on a petiole. In the juvenile phase, they are usually sessile, sitting directly on the shoot and in opposite pairs. In some, the juvenile foliage is a bright glaucous blue, much loved for flower arrangements. The time of flowering varies with the weather but it generally occurs in midsummer.

In the garden, eucalyptus make excellent and fast-growing specimen trees. They resent being transplanted – buy small, container-grown plants and never try to make

Eucalyptus 'Debeuzeville'

them stand up by staking. Indeed, cut them back to half their height – if the regrowth still flops over, repeat the cutting back.

KEY FACTS

Soil Perfectly happy in any soil, including acidic sands and chalky sites

Site Must have sun!

Height Smaller varieties 6m (20ft); others 10m (33ft)

Spread Smaller varieties 2m (6½ft); others 5m (16½ft)

Interest Fast-growing, specimen tree, evergreen, interesting bark and foliage often aromatic

Eucalyptus glaucescens

CARE: Can be reduced at almost any time, having an amazing ability to make new growth. Plant young saplings from pots when they are small; they can be coppiced if they are not stable. Can become prone to phytophthora root rot. Silver leaf can also affect eucalyptus.

EUCRYPHIA

These have large white flowers with a showy boss of stamens in mid- to late summer. This genus has both bush and tree forms. They have two main seasons, one lasting all year as they are evergreen, with the flowers also lasting for several weeks. The forms that make upright trees include *Eucryphia nymansensis* and *E. intermedia*. All the forms appreciate being shaded and kept cool at the roots, but with as much light as possible for the crown. In more temperate climates, they need protection from cold dry winds.

KEY FACTS

Soil Well-drained, moisture-retentive acid/neutral
Site Sun for the top, side shelter and shade for the roots
Height Dwarf 2m (6½ft); others 4m (13ft)
Spread Dwarf 1m (3ft); others 3m (10ft)
Interest Evergreen; white flowers

Eucryphia intermedia 'Rostrevor'

CARE: No special pruning regime is required; it can be reduced for size and reshaping. Protect from cold dry winds. Relatively trouble-free.

EUONYMUS

Spindle tree

Euonymus make small trees or shrubs. There are deciduous and evergreen species – and many of them provide excellent autumn colour. The late-spring flowers are rather nondescript, usually greenish yellow but some of them have a touch of purple or white. The fruit appears from autumn to winter and ripens to yellow-green or pink.

Euonymus can be used as specimen plantings, in a border or even as a screen.

KEY FACTS

Soil Well-drained soils of good to moderate fertility, especially good on shallow chalk

Site Sun or dappled shade

Height 3m (10ft)

Spread 3m (10ft)

Interest The foliage, autumn colour and ornamental fruits

Euonymus europaeus 'Red Cascade'

CARE: No pruning necessary except when reshaping or resizing is required. Fairly easy to manage and cultivate. Mulch to maintain humus content in soil. Occasionally caterpillars pay a visit and can cause slight damage.

FAGUS

Beech

Beech has a number of uses in the garden. Specimen trees give shape, colour and texture. Mature beeches form rounded domed crowns, usually as broad as they are high. However, the Dawyck beech (*Fagus sylvatica* 'Dawyck') has a narrow columnar crown, very reminiscent of the Lombardy poplar but a little broader. Beech foliage often contains large quantities of xanthocyanins, which give the tree its purple foliage. Another attractive feature of beech is the wonderful, fresh green new foliage, with the leaves turning russet colours in autumn. The silvery grey bark is also quite stunning. Most bark cells live for only a few years before dying, but in beech the cells in the bark can live for 100 years or more.

Fagus sylvatica 'Purple Fountain'

The other major use of beech is as a hedging plant. It can be trimmed to almost any height. Because trimming makes the foliage juvenile, a beech hedge will retain the old dead leaves until they drop off in spring when the buds expand.

KEY FACTS

Soil Any well-drained soil – beech will not tolerate waterlogging or heavy soils

Site Likes a site with both sun and medium, but not complete, shade

Height 4m (13ft)

Spread 3m (10ft)

Interest Stunning foliage with good autumn colour; attractive bark. Spring-flowering. Beech can also be used as hedging

Fagus sylvatica
'Dawyck Purple'

CARE: Clip hedges in late summer. Old plants do not respond to severe pruning. Beech is surface rooting so can be aggressive on other plants. It also casts a dense shade where planted. Grey squirrels can cause damage to the bark of the stem and major branches; bracket fungi can rot the heartwood.

FICUS

Fig

This large genus contains about 800 species, mainly evergreen trees, shrubs and woody climbers that flower in spring. In warmer climates use as specimen trees and train climbing species up walls.

For the garden, the fig of commerce (*Ficus carica*) is hardy and will ripen its fruits. It is deciduous with large, deeply lobed leaves on stout shoots. The fruits can take longer than a year to ripen. Two flushes are usually produced. The early summer flush invariably fails over winter, but the later flush is much smaller and hardier, and it is these that expand and ripen in late summer the following year.

Ficus carica
'Brown Turkey'

KEY FACTS

Soil Any well-drained, including chalk
Site Sun to light shade
Height 2.5m (8ft)
Spread 2.5m (8ft)
Interest Its foliage and edible fruits

CARE: Thin to prevent the plant becoming too dense and overcrowded. The genus is susceptible to a few pests and diseases but nothing major.

FRAXINUS

Ash

Ashes are deciduous trees with pinnate leaves. They mainly form substantial trees suited as specimens for the largest gardens or as peripheral screening.

The common ash (*Fraxinus excelsior*) has pleasing foliage and habit but few flowers and only a yellow autumn colour in good years. However, the manna ash (*Fraxinus ornus*) makes a very floriferous tree at a young age and has considerable beauty when the foliage is obliterated by the white flowers.

KEY FACTS

Soil Any well-drained soil
Site Sunny position
Height Smaller varieties 3m (10ft); others 7m (23ft)
Spread Smaller varieties 2m (6½ft); others will reach 5m (16½ft)
Interest Specimen or screening trees; spring-flowering; some species have good autumn colour

Fraxinus ornus

CARE: No pruning is required. Ashes are gross feeders that will compete with choice plants. Old trees can suffer from wood-decay fungi.

FREMONTODENDRON

This small genus is grown for the bright yellow flowers. These are carried singly from axillary buds in the shoots. The first flush of flowers, in late spring, come from the buds in last summer's shoots, but later blooms are on the current season's extension growths. The season of flowering extends into the summer and, in warmer areas, the autumn. Fremontodendron can be wall shrubs or trees – they are tender so need the shelter of a wall. They should not be over-fed or planted on fertile soils, or they will produce foliage at the expense of flowers. Sadly, they are not long-lived.

KEY FACTS
Soil Well-drained soil
Site Full sun
Height 8m (25ft)
Spread 6m (20ft)
Interest Fast-growing; bright yellow flowers

Fremontodendron
'California Glory'

CARE: Prune only to restrict growth or to reshape. Fairly easy to cultivate and maintain. As a general rule, tie in any wayward branches. Relatively trouble-free.

GARRYA

Silk tassel tree

These evergreen shrubs or small trees are grown for the catkins in mid-winter through to early spring. The catkins are best on the male forms, hanging like silk tassels and brightening up what can be a rather gloomy time of the year. The catkins are green with yellow anthers. *Garrya* can be damaged by cold dry winds in winter, so benefits from the shelter of a wall in cold areas. The catkins develop into deep purple-brown fruits, providing interest in autumn. However, apart from flowering time, *Garrya* can be rather dull.

KEY FACTS

Soil Well-drained soils of moderate fertility
Site Prefers a sunny to shady position – good for more temperate aspects
Height 3m (10ft)
Spread 3m (10ft)
Interest Showy catkins, fruits give autumn interest

Garrya elliptica

CARE: No pruning routine but, if necessary, prune after flowering. Fairly easy to maintain and cultivate. Any winter damage can be cut out and tidied up. Relatively trouble-free.

GINKGO

Ginkgo or maidenhair tree

This deciduous tree is assigned to a position between the ferns and the conifers in the evolutionary family tree. However, it is usually treated as an honorary conifer. Gingko is remarkably tough and tolerant of all forms of pollution – for example, two of the trees growing close to the centre of the nuclear blast at Hiroshima survived!

The leaves are fan-shaped and have an oily texture; an extract of the leaves is used as a health tonic. The seeds are tasty, but come with a drawback – the female fruit is surrounded by a stinking oily layer! The habit is generally narrow in young trees, only really broadening at around 100 years but by 250 years old, the crown is much broader.

The chief reason for planting gingko in the garden is the outstanding golden yellow autumnal colour, which has a clarity lacking in most other trees. The leaves hang on the trees for several weeks in mid- to late autumn. It also make an excellent specimen tree, flowering in spring.

If you are growing ginkgo for its fruit, it will be necessary to plant both sexes, or to graft a male branch onto a female tree.

KEY FACTS

Soil Any well-drained soil is fine, even less than satisfactory soils

Site For best results put gingko in the sun or light shade

Height 4m (13ft)

Spread 2m (6½ft)

Interest Great autumn colour, an excellent specimen tree. Gingko can also be grown for its fruit

Ginkgo biloba

CARE: Does not have a strict pruning regime, but will regrow if cut back. Very easy to cultivate and take care of; especially excellent in urban areas because it tolerates pollution. Does not have any particular problems with pests and diseases.

GLEDITSIA   *Honey locust or black locust*

This is a genus of legumes that have the characteristic legume pod. The foliage is variable; it is usually doubly pinnate with each of the leaflets (there can be up to eight of them) divided into about eleven pairs of very small leaflets. However, if less vigorous, it may only be pinnate, with 7–18 pairs of undivided leaflets. More confusingly, both leaf types can occur on the same leaf. The net result is very fine foliage,

which gives the tree a hazy appearance unless you are viewing it up close.

The spines of *Gleditsia triacanthos*, so-named because of the three-pronged spines, really are quite lethal, so thornless forms have been cultivated. 'Sunburst' has leaves that are golden yellow into summer when they change to a fresh green, before turning in the autumn to a warm gold colour before falling. 'Rubylace' has leaves that open wine red, greening in midsummer before giving autumn tints. Both of these forms will make small to medium trees over 30 or more years. In the garden they are useful as specimen trees, and for providing fresh colour.

KEY FACTS

Soil Grows best in acidic sands to alkaline soil but requires good drainage

Site Sunny sites – does not tolerate much shade

Height 5m (16½ft)

Spread 4m (13ft)

Interest Grown for its elegant form and very fine foliage. A good specimen tree

CARE: When pruning off branches, late summer is best as it reduces the risk of bleeding. A very easy tree to care for and cultivate that is relatively trouble-free.

Gledista triacanthos 'Sunburst'

HALESIA

Snowdrop tree

Halesia has white bell-shaped flowers in late spring as the leaves are expanding. The flowers hang down under last summer's growth. *Halesia* are much underused deciduous trees and shrubs.

Halesia monticola is the largest-growing of the species, likely to attain 10m (33ft) in 30 years, and is a good choice for a small ornamental tree. In some forms the flowers have a rose tinge. *Halesia caroliniana* is a smaller tree or spreading shrub, attaining 6m (20ft) in 30 years but twice as wide. The

fruit provides interest after the flowers have faded. It is hard and woody but has four wings running along the full length, and an awl-like projection at the tip. Initially green, the fruit is light brown when ripe.

The seeds can be slow to germinate, as they need a warm period in autumn to break down the hard, woody coat and then a cold winter period to stimulate germination. Cuttings of the new growths with a heel taken in late spring should root, but the resulting plants will need over-winter protection to get them through to next year.

KEY FACTS

Soil Performs well in moist, well-drained acidic to neutral soils
Site *Halesia* will grow equally well in both the sun or moderate shade
Height 6m (20ft)
Spread 5m (16½ft)
Interest Late spring-flowering tree that is grown for its white, bell-shaped flowers, winged fruits and autumn colour

CARE: No special pruning needed. However, if reducing a tree, prune after flowering. Easy to maintain. Mulch to maintain humus content in the soil and conserve soil moisture. Relatively trouble-free.

Halesia monticola f. *vestita*

HAMAMELIS

Witch hazel

Witch hazels are the source of the preparation used in eye lotions, which is distilled from the twigs. In the garden, however, their use is as winter-flowering shrubs or small trees. The first form of *Hamamelis intermedia* can be in bloom well before early/mid-winter, and the season extends right into early spring. The flowers of *H. intermedia* and *H. mollis* are carried on the bare, leafless branches. The petals are long and very narrow, and will tolerate extreme weather conditions. The flowers are also fragrant, especially in *H. mollis*. They are generally yellow, but in 'Jelena' the flowers give the impression of being a bright copper orange due to the base of the petal being red and the tip, yellow ochre.

The autumn colour of the hazel-like foliage is generally a rich yellow. However, with *Hamamelis vernalis* 'Sandra' the leaves turn orange, scarlet and red. The new foliage of this plant is suffused with a plum-purple, before becoming green with a purplish tinge to the underside.

Hamamelis make large shrubs or small trees, attaining 4–6m (13–20ft) and as wide or wider in around 20 or so years. The habit is generally open, which helps display the flowers.

KEY FACTS

Soil Neutral to acidic, humus-rich soils, or deep soils overlying chalk or limestone

Site Sun to medium shade. Shelter from cold, drying winds if possible

Height 4m (13ft)

Spread 4m (13ft)

Interest Good autumn colour; fragrant, spider-shaped yellow flowers also appear in summer and autumn

Hamamelis intermedia '**Pallida**'

CARE: No pruning needed, except to reshape or restrain; can be difficult to break from old wood. Mulch to maintain soil moisture and humus. Watch out for suckers on grafted plants. Relatively trouble-free. Does not have any particular problems with pests and diseases.

Hibiscus

HIBISCUS

Woody mallow

Lots of mallow-type flowers (with the stamens attached to the style) carried from spring to early autumn characterise these deciduous and evergreen shrubs and trees, provided they are given a warm and sunny position in the garden. The flowers are generally some form of blue, white or pink. The typical flower has a single row of five petals, which appear to form a trumpet; there are also double and semi-double flowers.

Hibiscus syriacus 'Hamabo'

KEY FACTS

Soil *Hibiscus* will grow in any well-drained soil, including chalky ones and acidic sands

Site Sun

Height 2.5m (8ft)

Spread 2m (6½ft)

Interest Grown for the showy flowers that last from spring right through the autumn

CARE: To maximise flower production, prune back last season's growth in late winter to the main branch structure. Mulch to protect the roots, especially in cold areas, and to maintain a high humus content in the soil. Fairly trouble-free.

IDESIA

Idesia has several attractive attributes that can enhance any garden. The most important has to be the large, heart-shaped leaves. The flowers are pale yellow and strongly fragrant. They are carried in early to midsummer in erect or pendulous panicles. Provided there is a male to pollinate them, these are succeeded on female trees by orange-red berries. These ripen in the autumn and persist after leaf fall. *Idesia* can make a sizeable tree with time but flowers at a young stage if planted in a hot, sunny position.

KEY FACTS

Soil Happy in any well-drained soil, including shallow soils over chalk
Site Will perform in a hot, sunny site
Height 5m (16½ft)
Spread 4m (13ft)
Interest Large, heart-shaped leaves, fragrant flowers, orange-red berries

Idesia polycarpa

CARE: No special pruning regime required, except to restrict or reshape. Fairly easy to cultivate and maintain. Needs both male and female plants for good fruiting. No particular problems with pests and diseases.

ILEX *Holly*

There are over 400 holly species, including both deciduous and evergreen species. Hollies are valuable as fruiting trees. The late-spring flowers are small, whitish-green and only of merit as the precursor of the fruit. This is only carried on female trees, although *Ilex aquifolium* 'J.C. van Tol' is hermaphrodite and will fruit on its own. Planting both sexes is important; however, you cannot go wrong if you plant *Ilex altaclerensis* 'Golden King' and either *Ilex aquifolium* 'Golden Queen' or 'Silver Queen' – strangely, the 'King' is female and the 'Queen' male! The berry is generally red, although *Ilex aquifolium* 'Bacciflava' has heavy crops of bright yellow berries.

Hollies are also valuable for their foliage, perhaps more so, as the berries last a few months (depending on how many birds you are feeding) but the foliage is evergreen. There are now many variegated forms; these have leaves that are creamy white, creamy yellow or gold to a greater or lesser degree.

In the garden, hollies are used as specimen trees and to make dense screens. They make excellent hedges, requiring clipping only once a year. They are also extremely shade tolerant, and are naturally under-storey trees.

KEY FACTS

Soil *Ilex* is extremely unfussy and will perform in any type of soil

Site Thrives in both sun and fairly dense shade

Height 3.5m (11½ft)

Spread 2m (6½ft)

Interest Good fruiting trees that are also grown for their foliage. Can be used for hedging

Ilex aquifolium
'Golden Queen'

CARE: Best pruned before new growth in late spring, but will tolerate pruning at any time. *Ilex* is very easy to maintain. Industrial pollution and maritime exposure will not affect its growth. Leaf miners can be a small problem but reasonably unaffected by pests and diseases.

JUGLANS

Walnut

Walnuts are grown in gardens partly for their nuts. They can be pickled whole, provided they are picked before the shell has become hard and woody, normally sometime around the second month of summer. They are even tastier if left to mature as walnuts, although squirrels like them at some intermediate stage and will quite merrily attempt to devour the lot. The outer case of the nut is green but gives a strong yellow dye that stains the hands. The flowers open with the new leaves in late spring and are susceptible to spring frost damage at this stage.

Walnuts also make bold foliage trees, with large pinnate leaves, and an attractive furrowed bark – shiny grey in *Juglans regia*, dark brown or black in *Juglans nigra*. The timber is excellent, with a dark heartwood and a fine grain.

In gardens, walnuts can only be planted as specimen trees. They need plenty of space and if given side shelter will become lanky. The roots give off chemicals that are toxic to many other plants, thereby reducing competition for water and nutrients. They thrive on all normal, well-drained soils, but with a bias towards soils of a more alkaline nature. *Juglans regia* needs excellent drainage; *J. nigra* a more moist soil.

KEY FACTS

Soil Happy in most normal, well-drained soils
Site Performs at its best in a hot, sunny position
Height 6m (20ft)
Spread 3m (10ft)
Interest Bold specimen trees with attractive bark that produce nuts. Some have good autumn colour

Juglans nigra

CARE: Only prune during summer, otherwise there is a risk of heavy bleeding. Apart from looking distressing, this can seriously weaken the tree as the sap contains reserves of sugars. Does not associate with many other garden plants because of toxic substances produced by the roots. Relatively trouble-free.

JUNIPERUS

Juniper

The junipers range from prostrate shrubs to tall trees 20m (65ft) high and 1m (3ft) in diameter. The characteristic that separates evergreen, coniferous junipers from the various cypresses is their fruit. Juniper berries are used as flavours in cooking and also to make London gin. They take one to three years to ripen, depending upon the species. They are even slower to germinate, taking up to five years, although most come up in the second spring.

Juniperus scopulorum 'Skyrocket'

KEY FACTS

Soil Prefers well- to moderately well-drained soil
Site Sun, but *J. chinensis* 'Aurea' has a deeper colour in dappled shade
Height 3m (10ft)
Spread Narrow forms 0.6m (2ft); others can spread 2.5m (8ft)
Interest Tall tree; produces berries

CARE: Can be clipped; will regrow from bare wood if not too much foliage removed. Generally these trees are rather prickly, so are best planted from pots as they do not transplant well. Leaf fungi and aphids can cause some problems; also can be susceptible to honey fungus.

LABURNUM

This yellow-flowered tree flowers in late spring or early summer with pendulous racemes. The flowers show its membership of the pea family, as does the fruit. Laburnum seeds are poisonous if eaten (as is the rest of the plant), although records of anyone being poisoned are extremely rare. The leaves are trifoliate, shiny green and may turn yellow in autumn. They make small trees, 5–8m (16½–25ft) and as much in spread. Use them as specimens trees, or as a larger item in a shrub or mixed bed. They can be trained over a pergola so that the flowers hang down below the structure.

Laburnum wateri 'Vossii'

KEY FACTS

Soil Will grow in any type of soil
Site Prefers sun to light shade
Height 5m (16½ft)
Spread 5m (16½ft)
Interest Grown for the pea-like, yellow flowers

CARE: No pruning necessary. Remove seed pods after flowering. Relatively trouble-free. No particular problems with pests and diseases.

LARIX

Larch

The larches are the largest genus of deciduous conifers. They have narrow columnar-conic crowns (except old trees, which are broader). The new foliage is an attractive green and the flowers, especially the female cone flowers, are bright red, pink or less often greenish-yellow and are carried from a young age. Then there is the autumn colour – yellow or orange. One-year-old twigs are brightly coloured too. In the garden they are used as specimen trees, for shelter plantings or as supports for climbing plants.

Larix decidua

KEY FACTS

Soil Well-drained, heavy; best on acidic/neutral soil
Site Sun; larches definitely don't like to be in any shade at all
Height 6m (20ft)
Spread 2.5m (8ft)
Interest Attractive young foliage, vibrant spring flowers and brilliant autumn colour

CARE: No pruning required, but the plant can be lightly reshaped. Larches are quick-growing and should be planted as small plants. Generally fairly trouble-free.

LAURUS

Bay laurel

Bay laurel is used as a herb in cooking and has aromatic leaves. Although often grown as a shrub *Laurus* will make an evergreen tree to 10m (33ft) or more in sunny, hot and fertile sites in mild climates. The flowers are creamy yellow and carried in late spring. They add brightness but are not exactly colourful. They are followed by black berries.

Laurus nobillis

In the garden, bay laurel is useful for its dense evergreen habit, and as a trimmed shrub in the kitchen garden. It can also be used as a hedging plant in milder countries, and is excellent for this in coastal areas. Bay laurel grows well in pots and can be clipped as topiary.

KEY FACTS

Soil Well-drained, fertile and preferably moist soil
Site Prefers sun; no more than dappled shade
Height 3.5m (11½ft)
Spread 2.5m (8ft)
Interest Aromatic leaves; good specimen tree, hedge or topiary

CARE: No special pruning regime is needed but very tolerant of clipping or coppicing. It puts out suckers from the stump and these may need removing to keep the habit neat. Relatively trouble-free.

Laurus nobilis

LIGUSTRUM

Privet

Privets are usually encountered as hedges, for which they do an excellent if uninspired job. The forms of *Ligustrum ovalifolium* are particularly useful in the hedging role, where their semi-evergreen foliage provides density to the screen in winter. The flowers of this common privet are in conical terminal panicles in midsummer. The Chinese privet, *Ligustrum lucidum*, is in a different class to all the others. This makes a small to medium specimen tree, eventually reaching 10m (33ft) or so, and has large, glossy leaves. It is also valuable for its flowers in early autumn.

KEY FACTS

Soil Well-drained to heavy soils
Site Sun to moderate shade
Height 3.5m (11½ft)
Spread 2m (6½ft)
Interest Foliage and flowers. Useful as hedging, some are good specimen trees

Ligustrum lucidum **'Excelsum Superbum'**

CARE: Light clipping or coppicing needed; trim hedges of *L. ovalifolium* 2–3 times each year. Easy to maintain and grow. Various insects can cause small leaf problems; more seriously, honey fungus can progressively kill a hedge.

LIQUIDAMBAR

Sweet gum

This small group of trees are usually grown for the maple-like leaves, which turn wonderfully in autumn, giving displays of orange, scarlet, red or crimson that last for two or more weeks.

Liquidambar styraciflua 'Silver Icing'

Sweet gum makes a good specimen tree wherever there is enough space for it to grow. If it reaches full maturity it may grow 25m (80ft) high, but that would take a century or so.

KEY FACTS
Soil Heavy, wet sites and well-drained loams
Site Prefers sun
Height 5m (16½ft)
Spread 2m (6½ft)
Interest Maple-like foliage with great autumn colour

CARE: No special pruning regime required, except to restrict or reshape. Fairly easy to cultivate and maintain. Relatively trouble-free. Does not have any particular problem with pests and diseases.

LIRIODENDRON

Tulip tree

The flowers on *Liriodendron* are like upright tulips, with six green-white petals that have an orange basal blotch (hence the common name). They are carried at the end of the leafy growths – formed from the previous summer's buds – on branchlets in the outer crown. The fruit is a woody cluster of samaras that persists over much of the winter as brown candles, before breaking apart to release the seeds. The flowers are attractive in their way but usually only produced on older trees out of sight of the ground. The leaves are more interesting – they have two side lobes but the tip is scalloped as if a giant caterpillar has removed a bite from the end. They also turn a beautiful golden yellow in autumn providing really excellent autumn colour.

Tulip trees make tall-growing specimens, up to 25m (80ft) on good sites over a century or so. Young trees have narrow columnar-conic crowns; in older trees, the crowns are broad columnar or domed. Locate them where they can be viewed from a window if you want to fully enjoy the flowers, and where the autumn colour is best displayed.

Liriodendron tulipferum

KEY FACTS
Soil Fertile, rich, well-drained to moist soils, including chalky ones
Site Prefers to be in the sun
Height 7m (23ft)
Spread 3m (10ft)
Interest Tulip trees are grown for their habit as well as the curiously shaped leaves that provide autumn colour

Liriodendron tulipiferum 'Aureomarginatum'

CARE: No special pruning regime required, except to restrict or reshape. Mulch and avoid activities that may compact the soil around the tree. Relatively trouble-free.

LUMA

Orange-bark myrtle

This evergreen tree is so amazing that it should be a good enough reason for moving to a mild region with high rainfall (the conditions it favours). The orange- or cinnamon-coloured bark cracks to reveal white streaks in older trees and is quite stunning.

The newly exposed bark of *Luma* has a velvety texture. The leaves are small, shiny green with an apiculate (shortly pointed) tip and are aromatic if crushed. The flowers are carried singly in the leaf axils at the tips of the current year's growths in late summer or early autumn. However, the shoot tips tend to have a large number of short nodes, giving a more clustered appearance to the flowers. They

Luma apiculata

Luma

have four white petals and many stamens. The fruit is a globose fleshy berry that is dark purple when ripe.

Unfortunately, this lovely tree is not winter cold hardy in inland sites. Even with woodland shelter or when grown on the side of a house it is liable to be cut back by hard winters before attaining a size that displays the colourful bark. However, in milder areas, it is a really first-class, narrow-crowned tree. It can also be clipped to make hedges.

KEY FACTS
Soil *Luma* enjoys any well-drained, moist soil that is rich in organic matter
Site This tree prefers a sunny position or can be situated in a woodland shelter
Height 4m (13ft)
Spread 2.5m (8ft)
Interest Grown for its stunning bark, aromatic leaves and cup-like flowers

Luma apiculata

CARE: No pruning required, except to remove any winter cold damage in late spring. Mulch to maintain the humus content in the soil and also to protect the root system against a cold winter. *Luma* does not have any particular problems with pests and diseases.

MAGNOLIA

Cultivated magnolia can be conveniently divided into two groups: those that flower on the bare shoots before the leaves and those which bear their flowers at the end of leafy shoots of the current year's growth.

Precocious-flowering magnolia

Precocious magnolia are those that flower in spring, on the bare boughs from large flower buds formed during the previous summer. The flowers are very conspicuous but are susceptible to frost damage so avoid frost pockets and cold-facing aspects.

Magnolia 'Iolanthe'

The taller forms carry their blooms high up, so are much more attractive if they can be seen from above. These magnolia range in size from the relatively slow-growing *Magnolia stellata*, which may make 3m (10ft) by 4m (13ft) in 30 years, to *M. campbellii* and its forms, which could reach 30m (100ft) in 50–80 years.

Later-flowering magnolia

These magnolia belong to quite separate groups but all flower on new leafy shoots. The commonest species in cultivation is *M. grandiflora* and its forms. They bear enormous, fragrant white flowers from early summer until the autumn frosts appear.

Magnolia loebneri
‘Leonard Messel’

KEY FACTS

Soil Well-drained acidic/neutral
Site Prefers sun to light overhead shade and moderate side shade
Height Small ones 2.5m (8ft); tall 8m (25ft)
Spread 4m (13ft)
Interest Showy, fragrant flowers

CARE: No pruning needed. If reshaping or restricting, prune after flowering. Mulch and do not disturb the soil under the crown spread or you will damage the fleshy roots that are close to soil surface. Relatively trouble-free.

MAHONIA

Mahonia have large pinnate leaves and larger-growing forms make excellent small, flowering trees over 15 to 20 years. The fragrant, yellow flowers are carried over winter. Individually, the flowers are small but are carried in a cluster of long racemes. The fruit is a blue-black berry that ripens in spring. Mahonia are ideal as framework plants in a shrub or mixed border, or in a woodland garden for their winter flowering and as specimen shrubs. They can also be used to make thick hedges and screens.

KEY FACTS

Soil Any type of well-drained soil, including chalky
Site Prefers sun but will tolerate moderate shade
Height 2.5m (8ft)
Spread 2m (6½ft)
Interest Handsome foliage, fragrant flowers, decorative berries

Mahonia japonica 'Bealei'

CARE: Pruning is only needed to restrict or reshape; mahonia will coppice freely. Fairly easy to maintain and cultivate. Remove any winter damage to the foliage in spring. Relatively trouble-free.

MALUS

Crab apple

These relatives of the domestic apple are floriferous small trees. They are particularly effective in late spring when the massed flowers smother the new foliage. They are grown for their often fragrant flowers and for their attractive, edible fruits, although some of the varieties produce fruits that are extremely unpalatable if uncooked.

Malus 'Evereste'

Some species can be effective for autumn colour, especially *Malus tschonoskii*, whose leaves turn a mixture of golds and scarlets, and *Malus transitoria* whose leaves turn a warm yellow. The new foliage can also provide interest.

Crab apples provide features of interest in the garden for much of the year. They make excellent small specimen trees for lawns or the larger shrub beds. They can be trimmed to make flowering hedges.

KEY FACTS

Soil Heavy to well-drained soils, including clays and chalky soils

Site Crab apples prefer to be in sun to light shade

Height 6m (20ft)

Spread 6m (20ft)

Interest Grown for their mass of flowers and attractive, edible fruits

CARE: No pruning is needed, but thin crowded crowns and remove defective or crossing branches. This plant does not require a lot of care and attention. For grafted trees, remove any suckers from the rootstock. Fruit tree pests and disease can affect crab apples, so keep a watchful eye out for these on the fruit and take quick action.

MESPILUS

Medlar

The medlar is a small tree whose origins lie in central and eastern Europe. On short, leafy shoots it carries single white flowers 2.5–4cm (1–1½in) across. These look similar to some of the less common *Crataegus* (*see* p.68) and, like this genus, it has short spines on the stronger shoots.

In flower the plant is quite attractive but not outstanding. The fruit, however, is unique. It is apple-shaped with a flat end, and has five large persistent stipules about 2.5cm (1in) long. The flesh is hard and inedible until it has been bletted. (This is a stage of incipient decay when the flesh becomes soft and sweet. Sounds horrid but the end result is very tasty.) The fruits are best left on the tree until mid-autumn or even later (frost assists bletting). The cultivar 'Nottingham' has rather tasty fruits and is less thorny with larger leaves, flowers and fruits. In autumn the leaves turn russet.

CARE: No special pruning regime required, except to restrict or reshape. Fairly easy to look after. Remove any suckers from the rootstock and beware of the thorns. A leaf blotch fungus can cause flowers to become sterile; also mildew can affect the foliage.

In the garden, medlar is useful as a small tree with a wide, spreading habit. Apart from its use in the orchard, it makes an interesting specimen tree for a lawn area or wild garden.

KEY FACTS

Soil Any well-drained soil, including clay and chalky

Site Flowering and fruiting much better in full sun, although it does tolerate light shade

Height 5m (16½ft)

Spread 5m (16½ft)

Interest Good specimen tree that has unusual, edible fruits

Mespilus germanica **'Nottingham'**

METASEQUOIA

Dawn redwood

Metasequoia glyptostroboides is one of the most graceful of conifers and makes a fast-growing deciduous tree that turns from yellow-brown through pink to red-brown in autumn. The habit is conical, becoming more columnar in older trees. The bark is orange-brown or red-brown, smooth at first then fibrous and stringy on the ridges. In the garden it can be used as a specimen tree, being especially effective around or in a (shallow) pond for its reflection.

Metasequoia glyptostroboides

KEY FACTS

Soil Any, although the very best growth is on fertile, moist to damp soils. It will happily grow in shallow water, albeit more slowly

Site Sun

Height 4m (13ft)

Spread 1.5m (5ft)

Interest This is a fast-growing specimen tree with excellent habit and interesting bark

CARE: No pruning needed. When grown on dry soils, it will appreciate water in summer. Fairly trouble-free from most pests and diseases.

MORUS

Mulberry

White mulberry (*Morus alba*) is important as the preferred food of the silkworm moth, whose caterpillar produces silk. The mulberry bushes are coppiced and the leaves stripped by hand and fed to the caterpillars. When mature, the caterpillars spin their pupal case and the thin threads of silk are unwound from this. White mulberry has glossy green foliage and makes a neat tree, but, apart from the silk industry, it is of limited horticultural value. Certainly the fruit, which is white or pink when ripe, is insipid. The form 'Pendula' has a weeping habit so that its branches form a small domed mound.

Horticulturally, the black mulberry (*Morus nigra*) is very superior. It forms an attractive small tree, which quickly develops a stout trunk. It also has a wonderfully tasty but tart

Morus alba 'Pendula'

Morus nigra

fruit. This ripens to purple-red (just edible at this stage) to dark purple-black (juicy and delectable) in mid- to late summer and into early autumn.

Apart from their culinary use, mulberries make neat specimen trees.

KEY FACTS
Soil Mulberries will tolerate most well-drained soils, including chalky ones
Site They will perform to their best if planted in sun
Height 5m (16½ft)
Spread 5m (16½ft)
Interest Good, small, spring-flowering specimen tree – *M. nigra* produces edible fruit

CARE: Avoid pruning unless really necessary as these trees may bleed. Be careful when first establishing – they have brittle roots and need careful handling when planting. Coral spot and mildew can cause occasional problems, but other than these they are fairly trouble-free.

NOTHOFAGUS

Southern beech

These late spring-flowering trees originate in the southern hemisphere. *Nothofagus dombeyi* is useful as a specimen tree, making a large and fast-growing evergreen – as does *N. obliqua*. The latter has bark that is smooth and grey in young trees, becoming shaggy with age, as it breaks into large scaly plates. Both can also be used for screening. *N. antarctica* is a deciduous species. It forms a small tree, so is the only one suitable for small gardens.

KEY FACTS

Soil Well-drained, acidic or neutral loams or soils
Site Performs to its best in sun
Height 8m (25ft)
Spread 4m (13ft)
Interest Habit and foliage; deciduous species have good autumn colour

Nothofagus obliqua

CARE: No pruning required, except to resize or reshape according to preference. Shelter from cold winds. *N. dombeyi* needs care when transplanting as leaves will wither if drought-stressed. Fairly trouble-free from pests and diseases, but could be susceptible to bark damage by squirrels.

NYSSA

Tupelo

Rightly or wrongly, these trees are grown for just one particular period of the year, lasting two to three weeks. This is when the foliage turns scrumptious colours in autumn, with brilliant shades of deep bright red, gold and scarlet. *Nyssa sylvatica* has glossy green foliage and makes a medium tree to 15m (50ft) or so in 40 years. It has a neat habit and is excellent

Nyssa sylvatica

beside water. *Nyssa sinensis* has richer autumn colour and larger leaves but they are not glossy like *N. sylvatica*. The habit is rounded with usually several stems, rather than the single-stemmed tree of *N. sylvatica*. Apart from the even more superior autumn colour, the advantage that *N. sinensis* has in many garden situations is that it is a smaller tree. This makes it better suited to modern gardens, where it is likely to make a tree 8–10m (25–33ft) in height over 40 years. The flowers are greenish and fairly insignificant, and are followed by blue-black berries – the main interest these have is to allow you to raise more!

KEY FACTS

Soil Performs best in acidic to neutral soils – avoid chalky ones
Site Does well in sun or dappled shade. Excellent beside water
Height 5m (16½ft)
Spread 2m (6½ft)
Interest Fantastic autumn colour; great specimen trees for growing near water

CARE: No pruning required except to resize or reshape according to preference. Can be difficult to establish, so use pot-grown trees of around 30–50cm (12–20in) in height. Does not have any real problems with pests and diseases.

Olea

OLEA

Olive

The olive must be the most characteristic tree of Mediterranean landscapes, and its fruits are the source of olive oil. The species is not reliably hardy and is not commonly cultivated in more temperate climates. Most olives seen are in pots but they can be grown in a bed outside in milder areas, especially if given the shelter of a wall. Olives have evergreen, grey-green leaves that are glaucous beneath. The flowers are in axillary racemes in late summer. They are small, white and fragrant. The fruit ripens from green to black over winter. They need full sun and a freely drained soil.

Olea europaea

KEY FACTS

Soil Any, as long as it is well-drained
Site Needs a sunny position
Height 3m (10ft)
Spread 2.5m (8ft)
Interest Produces edible fruit; olives

CARE: Prune to restrict size. No particular care regime is needed. Tolerates hot, dry sites in nature. Scale insects and verticillium wilt can affect them.

OSTRYA

Hop hornbeam

This tree is related to *Carpinus* (*see* p. 49), differing in that the male catkins are exposed in the bud stage over winter and the seed is entirely enclosed in the papery bladder. It forms a broad conical to columnar tree, with a single stem and level branching.

This particular shape of tree provides an excellent platform from which the yellow catkins are displayed. *Ostrya* makes attractive specimen trees for large gardens. The foliage looks especially attractive in the autumn when it turns a lovely shade of yellow.

KEY FACTS

Soil Any, as long as it is well-drained
Site A sunny position
Height 6m (20ft)
Spread 4m (13ft)
Interest Excellent specimen trees, attractive foliage, especially during the autumn

Ostrya virginiana

CARE: No pruning needed, except to restrict or reshape. No particular problems with pests and diseases.

Oxydendrum

OXYDENDRUM

Sorrel tree

This deciduous tree has white, fragrant, bell-shaped flowers in late summer or early autumn. The panicles, produced at the tips of the current season's growth, may be 15–25cm (6–10in) long. The leaves turn lovely shades of red and scarlet in autumn. The common name, sorrel tree, refers to the taste of the leaves.

Sorrel trees are capable of growing to 15m (50ft) after 50–80 years, but will only do this if grown in suitable woodland conditions. They tend only to be available as small nursery plants and are slow-growing. So, plan for them to grow to 5–8m (16½–25ft) and enjoy the autumn contribution while you wait.

Oxydendrum arboreum

KEY FACTS
Soil Acidic and well-drained
Site Sun is best
Height 3m (10ft)
Spread 2m (6½ft)
Interest Late flowers; autumn colour

CARE: No specific pruning regime is necessary. Mulch to keep the soil acidity and humus status. Does not have any particular problems with pests and diseases.

PARROTIA

Persian ironwood

This tree flowers on the bare branches in late winter or early spring. They have no petals but are showy due to the numerous deep red stamens. At this time of the year the bark, which peels to reveal pink-buff and yellow that darkens through grey-green to grey-brown, is also attractive.

The foliage is dense and glossy green, coming into its own in autumn when it turns red, orange and crimson before falling as deep red. *Parrotia* is useful as a specimen tree, in shrub borders or can be used in screening plantings.

KEY FACTS

Soil Needs well-drained, moisture-retentive soil
Site Sun to light shade
Height 3.5m (11½ft)
Spread 4m (13ft)
Interest Peeling bark, attractive foliage and petalless flowers

Parrotia persica

CARE: No specific pruning regime is necessary, but you can prune to give a clean stem. Does not have any particular problems with pests and diseases.

PAULOWNIA *Foxglove tree or empress tree*

This tree has delicately lilac-scented flowers that open in late spring. However, they are formed at the end of summer and are displayed as buds at the end of the stout shoots. The individual blooms are tubular in shape, like thimbles or foxglove blooms. The flowers can be damaged by late spring frosts. The leaves are large, verging on the enormous; they can be up to 60cm (2ft) across on young or coppiced trees, but are more usually 15–35cm (6–14in) by 10–25cm (4–10in). They are ovate with sticky,

Paulownia tomentosa

glandular hairs on the underside, and are very thin and easily shredded by strong winds. They remain green until felled by the first strong frost. They cast only a light to moderate shade and are late coming into leaf. This makes *Paulownia tomentosa* the most useful species for the garden as an over-storey tree above spring-flowering shrubs.

In the garden this plant is best grown as a specimen tree. The other way is to grow it as a foliage plant. Cut back an established plant growing in a well-manured spot to ground level in late winter and thin the new growth to a single stem. This will make 2.5m (8ft) by the autumn and will have leaves individually to 0.6m (2ft) across.

KEY FACTS

Soil Will grow in any well-drained soil, including clays and chalky ones

Site *Paulownia* prefers a warm, sunny position

Height 7m (23ft)

Spread 6m (20ft)

Interest These plants are grown for their habit, attractive foliage and showy, scented flowers

CARE: No pruning required except to remove winter damage and broken branches. Vigorous young shoots are pithy and liable to be cut back in winter by the cold. Relatively trouble-free. Does not have any particular problems with pests and diseases.

PHELLODENDRON

Cork bark tree

This tree is of interest for the pinnate leaves and the bark, which is corky in old trees. The leaves are aromatic and turn clear yellow in early autumn. The flowers are yellow-green and carried in early summer in large terminal panicles. On female trees, they are followed by pea-sized black fruits that may persist well into winter, depending on the mildness of the season. The fruits have a strong, citrus scent. Old trees develop an open branching habit and make picturesque specimen trees for large lawns.

Phellodendron amurense

KEY FACTS

Soil Well-drained soil, especially chalk
Site Sun or light shade
Height 6m (20ft)
Spread 4m (13ft)
Interest Attractive foliage, aromatic leaves, corky bark – female trees have scented fruits

CARE: No pruning needed, except to repair frost/other damage. Both male and female trees are needed for the fruit to be produced. Fairly trouble-free.

PHILLYREA

This evergreen shrub or tree has a rounded, domed crown with narrow dark green leaves, giving a dense leafy crown. The flowers are creamy white and fragrant, and carried in late spring and early summer from buds on last summer's growth. The fruit ripens in late summer and is blue-black, although only reliably produced in regions with fairly warm climates.

Phillyrea is an excellent small evergreen for the front garden where something reliable but unusual is desired. It can also be clipped as a hedge.

Phillyrea decora

KEY FACTS

Soil Well-drained soil; is especially good on shallow soils over chalk

Site This plant prefers to be in a sunny position

Height 3m (10ft)

Spread 2.5m (18ft)

Interest This is a good evergreen that also provides fragrant white flowers

CARE: Coppice if needed and remove any damaged shoots. There are no particular problems with pests and diseases.

PHOTINIA

This genus is noted for the large corymbs of white, hawthorn-like flowers and the small berries, which are like miniature apples. Most of the species are evergreen but they contain some of the most colourful of foliages. In *Photinia davidiana* the leaves are matt green and most persist through the winter. A few of its leaves do fall in autumn, displaying red or orange colours. A few more do the same over winter and most of the others follow in spring. Thus, while it does not have outstanding autumn colour, it does provide a protracted display. 'Palette' has blotched leaves that are streaked with creamy-white and have a pinkish tinge when new.

Photinia davidiana **'Palette'**

Photinia fraseri 'Red Robin' has foliage that flushes brilliant red, contrasting with the dark glossy green of last year's foliage. *Photinia serrulatifolia* (*Photinia serrulata*) can make a large tree with time and is a high-quality evergreen. The new foliage is often bronze or red for an extended period. The bark is grey-brown, exfoliating to reveal red-brown beneath. *Photinia davidiana* and *Photinia fraseri* 'Red Robin' are good in shrub beds and can be used as hedges. *Photinia serrulatifolia* must be positioned as a specimen tree.

KEY FACTS

Soil Any that is well-drained, including clays and chalky soils
Site Prefers a sunny position but is quite happy to tolerate light shade
Height 5m (16½ft)
Spread 4m (13ft)
Interest White hawthorn-like flowers in spring/summer and fruits like miniature apples. Good autumn colour

CARE: No special pruning regime is required except to restrict or reshape. *P. serrulatifolia* can be damaged by spring frosts so give winter protection when young, or plant by a wall. These trees are fairly trouble-free but can be susceptible to fireblight.

PICEA

Spruce

The spruces are narrow-crowned, evergreen trees. They are strongly monopodal, i.e. with a single main stem and only light side branching. The width can be as much as 4m (13ft) radius with most species when mature. The exception is *Picea omorika*, which even as a 25m (80ft) tall tree is only up to 1.5m (5ft) in diameter.

Picea orientalis is an attractive species for its short needles, its brick-red male cones in mid-spring and red female cone flowers, and its habit. The cultivar 'Aurea' has new foliage that is golden yellow before turning dark green and merging with the older leaves. *P. breweriana* is the most attractive of the common species. The leaves are dark, glossy green on the top side and silvery green on the underside. The habit is spectacular, with the side branches off the trunk festooned with long hanging and unbranched twigs up to 2m (6½ft) in length.

Picea abies

P. pungens is represented by blue foliage selections. The best colour is found on the one-year foliage and this contrasts with the dull green of older foliage.

KEY FACTS

Soil Well-drained, acidic to slightly alkaline; *P. omorika* tolerates more alkaline soils

Site These trees perform at their best in a situation that has full sun

Height 4.5m (15ft)

Spread 2m (6½ft)

Interest Evergreen, coniferous trees that are useful for shelter planting or specimens. Flowers appear in spring, and these are followed by cones

Picea pungens 'Hoopsii'

CARE: No pruning required; only lightly trim into existing foliage bearing shoots. Easy to cultivate. Grafted plants may need staking to get them to form an erect leader. Aphids can kill needles.

PINUS

Pine

Pines are intriguing for their evergreen foliage. The leaves or needles are in small clusters of between two and five, which, when fitted together, form a perfect cylinder. Flowering trees have male cones at the base, foliage in the middle and female cones at the tip of each 'node'. The larger-growing pines make good specimen trees in a garden. They can also be used as shelter or to form a backdrop to other plants.

Pinus sylvestris 'Fastigiata'

KEY FACTS

Soil Well-drained, especially acidic to neutral; *P. nigra* and *P. wallichiana* over chalk
Site Sun
Height 5m (16½ft)
Spread 5m (16½ft)
Interest Great specimen trees that have intriguing, evergreen foliage. Can also be used for sheltering

CARE: No special pruning regime required, except to remove damaged branches. Position is important as they need full side light to keep the lower branches healthy. Young trees can be killed by honey fungus, but apart from this they are fairly trouble-free.

PITTOSPORUM

This genus is distributed worldwide. The plants in this group are all evergreen shrubs and trees. In colder climates they can be damaged by hard winters but are excellent for coastal sites. *Pittosporum tenuifolium*, originating from New Zealand, is the main species in cultivation but a Chinese species, *Pittosporum tobira* is also common. Other more tender species are occasionally available but they may be lost in the next hard winter, except in milder gardens. The chief attractions are in the fragrant flowers and the foliage. The late spring/early summer flowers are chocolate-

Pittosporum tenuifolium 'Tom Thumb'

purple in *Pittosporum tenuifolium* and creamy-white in *Pittosporum tobira*. *P. tenuifolium*, in particular, has given a number of forms with attractive foliage, ranging from bronze-purple in 'Purpureum', to variegated foliage, which may be creamy-white, e.g. 'Irene Paterson', to gold in 'Warnham Gold'. There are also a number of slow-growing selections, of which 'Tom Thumb' is perhaps the smallest.

In the garden, the smaller forms are excellent as part of shrub beds, with the larger ones at the back. They can be sited beside house walls, especially in colder areas, and make good hedges. The largest forms are good specimen trees.

KEY FACTS

Soil Well-drained and fertile soils, acidic or alkaline
Site Full sun – tolerates a moderate amount of shade
Height Smallest varieties 1m (3ft); others 3m (10ft)
Spread Smallest varieties 0.6m (2ft); others 2m (6½ft)
Interest Attractive flowers and foliage; excellent for coastal sites

CARE: No special pruning regime required except to restrict or reshape. In colder gardens, *Pittosporum* will benefit from side or wall shelter. Mildew and tar spot fungi can be occasionally problematic but are not usually serious.

PLATANUS

Plane

Planes are large trees, characteristic of major open spaces in many cities. As free-growing trees they will make 25m (80ft) or more in a century, and can live for several hundred years. They are only suitable for the largest gardens as trees. However, they can have a role to play. The trees can be pleached, where the branches are woven to create a framework; the growths are cut back to this framework each winter. Vigorous regrowth quickly forms a dense canopy of foliage, giving good shade from early summer onwards.

KEY FACTS

Soil Well-drained; gravel, sand and clay
Site Grows well in full sun
Height 7m (23ft)
Spread 5m (16½ft)
Interest Very large tree with an open habit. Inconspicuous flowers in spring; fruits in winter

Platanus hispanica

CARE: Prune hard, or pollard in winter. The fine hairs on the fruits can cause dermatitis in some people. Anthracnose can cause the death of new foliage in wet springs, but later growth is unaffected.

PODOCARPUS

Foot yew

This genus contains a number of large trees, but most are too tender for more temperate conditions, and the hardier ones are small shrubs. *Podocarpus salignus* is hardy in cooler climates provided it has some side shelter in cold gardens, and it can make a very attractive evergreen tree. The foliage is somewhat yew-like, but much longer, to 10cm (4in). *Podocarpus totara* has shorter needles and makes a wider spreading tree with light, evergreen foliage.

They are attractive as a feature by themselves in the garden. The fruits are only formed if both male and female trees are present.

KEY FACTS

Soil Well-drained soil preferred

Site Sun to moderate shade

Height 3m (10ft)

Spread 2m (6½ft)

Interest Grown for its spirally arranged, yew-like leaves

Podocarpus salignus

CARE: Can be trimmed. Grows best with side shelter. Generally fairly trouble-free from most pests and diseases.

PONCIRUS

Japanese bitter orange

A spiny, deciduous shrub or small tree. The main attraction is in the large white and strongly fragrant flowers that are carried in spring. The fruit ripens in autumn and is a small, globose orange. The fruit is extremely bitter in taste. The leaves are trifoliate but are set on green stems that are provided with stout spines.

In the garden *Poncirus* is useful for the fragrant flowers and the all-year attraction of the green stems. Its spiny nature means it can be used to form barriers. As a hardy orange tree it is also used as a rootstock for grafting true oranges and lemons (*Citrus* sp).

KEY FACTS
Soil Well-drained; acidic or alkaline
Site Sun or dappled shade
Height 2.5m (8ft)
Spread 2m (6½ft)
Interest Large, scented white flowers in spring and orange-like fruit in autumn

Poncirus trifoliata

CARE: Trim after flowering or fruiting – but beware of the spines! Not usually affected by pests and diseases.

POPULUS

Poplar

The poplars are a genus of large trees. They grow vigorously on a wide range of soils, except shallow chalky ones where growth is less satisfactory. They are useful for their attractive foliage, be it the foliage of aspen (*Populus tremula*), which rustles in the wind due to a flattened petiole; the silvery undersides of the various forms of white poplar (*Populus alba*) or the large heart-shaped leaves of the Chinese necklace poplar (*Populus lasiocarpa*).

Poplars like plenty of soil moisture, although they are not trees for really

Populus lasiocarpa

boggy conditions. However, their fast growth rate coupled with a profligate use of water can cause subsidence problems on shrinkable soils, primarily clays, where foundations are inadequate. Generally it is best to keep poplars at least their height away from buildings – but if you are growing them on sand or loam you shouldn't have a problem.

KEY FACTS

Soil Performs well in any soil type, except very wet and boggy soils

Site Loves to be in a warm spot where it can get lots of sunshine

Height 7m (23ft); tall varieties can grow to 11m (36ft)

Spread 5m (16½ft)

Interest Due to their fast growth they are useful as big specimen trees. They are also grown for their very attractive foliage

CARE: No special regime required but they are very tolerant of pruning. Easy to cultivate and maintain. Branches are brittle and can be broken by strong winds. Cankers cause stem lesions on *P. jackii* 'Aurora'; fungi and insects attack them but without causing real harm.

PRUNUS

Cherry, plum

Prunus is such a diverse genus that it is often split into several genera. The cherries belong to the Cerasus group. The other species are members of the plum group, which retains the generic name *Prunus*; the bird cherry group or Padus; the almonds or Amygdalus and the cherry laurel group, Laurocerasus. The unifying feature of this genus is that the fruit is a drupe – a fruit in which the seed is enclosed by a hard stony layer surrounded by a fleshy layer.

Cerasus

The true cherries (Cerasus) are grown for the spring flowers, and often for the autumn colour of their foliage. The best colour, in early autumn, is provided by *Prunus sargentii*. The Tibetan cherry, *P. serrula*, is grown for the smooth polished mahogany bark. This group also includes the Japanese cherries.

Prunus lusitanica

Other groups

These include the almond (*Prunus dulcis*). The kernel of the fruits is edible in the sweet almonds but the bitter almonds contain a high concentration of prussic acid (can be lethal if too many are eaten). This acid is also found in the cherry laurel (*P. laurocerasus*), which can make a medium-sized tree. The cherry plum, *P. cerasifera*, is one of the earliest flowering and is used as an informal hedging plant. The bird cherries have racemes of flowers carried at the end of leafy shoots in spring.

KEY FACTS

Soil Any well-drained soil; best on deep heavy loams
Site Sun or light shade
Height Small varieties 3m (10ft); others 7m (23ft)
Spread Small varieties 3m (10ft); others 6m (20ft)
Interest Flowers, fruit – sometimes edible; some species have shiny, coloured bark; others have good autumn colour

CARE: Pruning is best done in midsummer, to reduce the risk of silver leaf infections. On chalky soils, *Prunus* can become chlorotic; improve leaf colour by watering with Epsom salts. Silver leaf disease can kill cherries; various leaf/petal fungi can kill leaves; aphids (blackfly) are also a problem.

PSEUDOLARIX

Golden larch

This genus contains only one species, *Pseudolarix amabilis*. *Amabilis* translates as 'lovely', and when in its autumn glory, this is an understatement. The leaves turn golden-orange before falling. The cones are spiky and fall apart to release the seeds.

Pseudolarix makes a spreading tree, ultimately as broad as tall. It is slow to get established, often making little growth in the first two to five years, but then speeds up. Use it as a specimen tree.

Pseudolarix amabilis

KEY FACTS

Soil Well-drained, preferably lime-free soil
Site Prefers full sun
Height 2.5m (8ft)
Spread 2m (6½ft)
Interest Great autumn colour; coniferous specimen tree

CARE: Prune only to remove dead branches. This tree is slow to get going, so keep it weed-free when young. It is generally fairly trouble-free from most pests and diseases.

PSEUDOTSUGA

Douglas fir

Pseudotsuga menziesii makes a large and fast-growing evergreen tree. It has an excellent reddish timber and is widely used in forestry. The forms with blue foliage, *Pseudotsuga menziesii* ssp. *glauca*, are very attractive, slower-growing and make smaller trees. The trunk develops a thick, corky, deeply ridged bark in old trees. In the garden, Douglas fir makes a specimen tree or can be used as part of a shelter planting. It will withstand exposure but will thrive much better if it is planted in a sheltered spot.

KEY FACTS

Soil Well-drained soil
Site Prefers sun, but will tolerate shade when young
Height 6m (20ft)
Spread 2m (6½ft)
Interest Imposing, coniferous specimen trees. Interesting ridged bark in older trees

Pseudotsuga menziesii

CARE: Avoid pruning if possible. Late spring frosts can cause damage and a needle-killing fungus can affect the leaves of blue forms.

PTELEA

Hop tree

These are small shrubby trees, rarely making more than 8m (25ft) and usually only 6m (20ft) over 30 years. They belong to the Rutaceae, the same family as oranges and lemons. All members of this family have small translucent glands in the foliage that make it aromatic if crushed. *Ptelea* are deciduous with trifoliate leaves. The summer flowers are greenish-white and are usually strongly scented. They are followed by the flattened winged fruits, which are similar to those of elm.

Ptelea trifoliata 'Aurea'

Ptelea can be sited in a shrub border, but are better as a specimen in a grassy area.

KEY FACTS
Soil Well-drained soil
Site Prefers a sunny position
Height 3.5m (11½ft)
Spread 2.5m (6½ft)
Interest Aromatic leaves and flowers

CARE: No special pruning regime required except to restrict or reshape. An extremely easy tree to cultivate and manage. Relatively trouble-free.

PYRACANTHA

Firethorn

Pyracantha are often grown as wall shrubs, free-standing shrubs and trees. They have two main seasons of display – early summer and autumn. In the early summer, the branches are smothered by clusters of white hawthorn-like flowers. These are followed in the autumn by berries, which are small apple-like fruits. The fruits ripen to red, orange or golden yellow. *Pyracantha* will withstand clipping and can be used to form topiaries or hedges. They are evergreens and can get damaged by cold dry winds in winter, so shelter from such weather is beneficial.

KEY FACTS

Soil Any well-drained soil
Site Sun or partial shade
Height 4m (13ft)
Spread 3m (10ft)
Interest Foliage, flowers and the showy fruit

Pyracantha 'Teton'

CARE: No hard pruning required. Clip to reshape or reduce after flowering. Check for dieback due to disease or insects and watch out for the sharp spiny thorns. Prone to the general diseases found on apples, including scab, fireblight, aphids and scale insects.

PYRUS

Pears are most often found in the orchard or as espaliers along the fence of the kitchen garden, where they are grown for their fruit. However, they are also very attractive in flower and include species that are well worth growing in the garden. The common pear is *Pyrus communis*, of which over 1,000 fruiting cultivars are recorded, ranging from dessert varieties to those intended for perry production (cider with pears).

Pyrus salcifolia 'Pendula'

The variety 'Beech Hill' is a form of common pear with small fruits about 2.5cm (1in) across; the branches are erect, giving a narrow crowned tree and the glossy green leaves turn a bright orange-yellow in autumn. *Pyrus calleryana* 'Chanticleer' has a similar habit – its flowers are white and carried in early spring. This tree is widely used as a street tree but its tough

Pyrus calleryana 'Chanticleer'

constitution, narrow ovoid habit and colourful flowers make it desirable for smaller gardens.

The most common amenity pear is the weeping form of *Pyrus salicifolia*, 'Pendula'. The narrow leaves are silvery-grey and the pendent branch habit makes a small, neat tree. It has white flowers, but these are rather lost against the foliage.

KEY FACTS
Soil Well-drained or moist but not wet. Preferably fertile soils
Site Likes lots of sun
Height 7m (23ft)
Spread 5m (16½ft)
Interest Usually grown for their fruit but also attractive in flower

CARE: No particular pruning regime, except to restrict or reshape; remove damaged and crossing branches. Fairly easy to cultivate and look after. Be careful to remove suckers from the rootstocks. They can get scab and fireblight, and other diseases of fruit trees but are generally healthy.

QUERCUS

Oak

Oaks are mainly large-growing trees so few are suitable for small gardens. The genus comprises several hundred different species. The smallest ones in general cultivation are two forms of common oak, *Quercus robur*: the Concord oak, *Q. robur* 'Concordia' and the Cypress oak, *Q. robur* 'Fastigiata'. Most other oaks are capable of making tall trees. This is especially true with Turkey oak (*Q. cerris*), scarlet oak (*Q. coccinea*), Hungarian oak (*Q. frainetto*), Pin oak (*Q. palustris*), sessile oak (*Q. petraea*), common oak (*Q. robur*) and red oak (*Q. rubra*).

Quercus rubra

KEY FACTS

Soil Heavy to well-drained soil
Site Likes lots of sun
Height Smallest 2.5m (8ft); others 7m (23ft)
Spread 4m (13ft)
Interest Habit and foliage; acorns

CARE: No pruning necessary, except to restrict or reshape; remove damaged and crossing branches. Easy to care for. Mildew can cause foliage loss but only serious in shade; various insects eat the foliage – rarely cause harm.

RHODODENDRON

This genus contains a wealth of attractive shrubs and trees, perhaps as many as 800 species and innumerable hybrids. The rhododendron that are discussed here are all capable of making large, evergreen shrubs or small trees, upwards of 4–5m (13–16½ft) in height.

Some of the species, such as *Rhododendron falconeri* and *R. fulvum*, have beautiful red-brown hairs in the underside of the leaves, and *R. falconeri* also has an attractive peeling bark. These require the shelter of a light woodland setting, but *R. makinoi*, with narrow leaves that have a white or tawny-white underside, will take a position in full sun.

The old 'Hardy Hybrids' combine several species in their parentage and were first developed in the 19th century. 'Gomer Waterer' has white flowers that are flushed mauve around the edges of the petals. 'Pink Pearl', with its conical trusses of deep lilac-pink, is very attractive, if somewhat garish, and fades as the flowers mature.

Although these plants will make large shrubs or small trees, they will only do so at a modest rate, growing roughly 20–30cm (8–12in) a year.

KEY FACTS

Soil Well-drained but moist, acidic soil

Site Sun to light shade

Height 2.5m (8ft)

Spread 2m (6½ft)

Interest Mainly grown for their spectacular, and sometimes scented, flowers, which appear in spring and/or summer. These range from white, yellow, pink to mauve

CARE: This plant benefits from the removal of spent flowers. Mulch using leafmould or peat. Relatively trouble-free – no particular problems with pests and diseases.

Rhododendron 'Pink Pearl'

ROBINIA

This is a genus of trees or large shrubs with pinnate leaves and showy, pea-like flowers. These are usually white but in *Robinia hispida* they are a deep rose colour. The shoots usually have two recurved spines, one on either side of the bud or leaf. *Robinia* are tolerant of urban conditions. The leaves fall without adopting any colour in autumn. In the garden, the bright foliage of *R. pseudoacacia* 'Frisia' makes an excellent golden-yellow tree.

Robinia pseudoacacia **'Frisia'**

KEY FACTS

Soil Any well-drained soil – not good for shallow chalk but excellent on sand

Site This plant is a sun lover

Height Small varieties 2m (6$\frac{1}{2}$ft); others 7m (23ft)

Spread Small varieties 2m (6$\frac{1}{2}$ft); others 5m (16$\frac{1}{2}$ft)

Interest Its leaves and flowers

CARE: No special pruning is required but can be trimmed to restrict growth. The stems are quite brittle and liable to snap during windy periods when in full leaf. Young trees are liable to grow too dense and heavy so prune in late summer. No particular problems with pests and diseases.

SALIX

Willow

The genus *Salix* is widely distributed, from moorland to thicket and forest, with species ranging from less than 2.5cm (1in) in height to 30m (100ft) or more. These plants are often associated with water, and the weeping willow, *Salix sepulcralis* 'Chrysocoma', is really good when reflected in a large lake.

Salix are extremely tolerant of being cut back. This is useful when keeping a large weeping willow in too small a garden or bringing out the best twig colour in *Salix alba* ssp. *vitellina* 'Britzensis'; the one-year shoots only develop the full bright orange-scarlet colour in mid-winter.

Salix gracillistyla 'Melanostachys'

Trees can be pollarded at 3–4m (10–13ft) or coppiced near ground level to maximise the production of colourful shoots, whether annually or better still on a two or three-year cycle. The catkins can be attractive but the two sexes occur on different trees; the male ones with their pollen-bearing anthers are generally more showy, especially at the silky hairy stage, than the green female catkins. The catkins of *Salix gracillistyla* 'Melanostachys' are almost black with brick-red anthers and yellow pollen. The smaller-growing species can be very attractive for their foliage, especially *Salix fargesii* and *Salix magnifica*.

KEY FACTS

Soil These trees like any type of soil, provided it is not too dry

Site *Salix* enjoy being situated in a warm and sunny part of the garden

Height Small species 4m (13ft); others 9m (30ft)

Spread 6m (20ft)

Interest Cultivated for their habit, especially weeping forms, catkins, foliage and some forms also have stunning winter shoots

CARE: Can be hard pruned, especially to produce osiers for basketry. Generally very easy to maintain and cultivate – they tend to look after themselves. Anthracnose is a fungal disease that kills the new foliage in wet springs but the plants will usually recover well from this.

SAMBUCUS

Elder

The elders are valuable for their flowers and fruit. Both can be used to make cordials. The flowers are carried in large, usually flat-topped trusses and are white or ivory-coloured. The fruits may be purple or red; they (like other parts of the plant) can be irritants but cooking removes this blemish. The foliage is pinnate, but drops without giving any colour in autumn. However, there are a number of selections with golden-yellow foliage that are great.

Sambucus racemosa 'Plumosa Aurea'

In the garden *Sambucus* can be used in shrub borders or as specimen trees. They can withstand shade and golden foliage forms can enliven dank corners.

KEY FACTS

Soil Any well-drained soil
Site Prefers sun but also some shade
Height 5m (16½ft)
Spread 5m (16½ft)
Interest Foliage, flowers and fruit

CARE: No specific pruning requirements, but can be hard pruned to restrict spread. Coloured foliage forms the best when it is situated in dappled shade. Relatively trouble-free.

SASSAFRAS

Sassafras albidum makes a small to medium-sized tree with an upright ovoid crown and is the best species for a woodland or fairly large garden. The leaves are ovate or obovate; most are entire but some have one or two deep rounded sinuses and conspicuous lobes. The leaves turn a rich yellow, orange or red in autumn. If crushed they are strongly aromatic, as are the green shoots, and if chewed have a spicy flavour that numbs the mouth. The yellow, discretely showy flowers are carried in spring. Fruits are only formed where male and female trees are grown; the fruits are dark blue and set on a red stalk.

KEY FACTS

Soil Any soil that varies from either acidic to neutral
Site Sun or light shade
Height 5m (16½ft)
Spread 4m (13ft)
Interest Stately habit and glossary, aromatic foliage

Sassafras albidum

CARE: No specific pruning regime is required, except to resize or reshape. Fairly easy to cultivate and maintain. It would benefit from some side shelter. Relatively trouble-free.

SAXEGOTHEA

Prince Albert yew

Saxegothea conspicua is named after Queen Victoria's consort, Prince Albert. It is not a yew but a podocarp relative. The foliage, though, is somewhat yew-like. It consists of a whorl of five or six side branches with a single extension shoot. This can make a tall tree with a narrow crown depending on climate – 15m (50ft) or so after 50 years in warm areas, and no more than a shrub 3m (10ft) tall in more temperate climes. It produces fleshy female cones and small male ones. In the garden, use it as a large, evergreen specimen narrow-crowned tree or as part of a shrub bed.

Saxegothea conspicua

KEY FACTS

Soil Well-drained, acidic or lightly alkaline soil
Site This particular plant is definitely a sun lover
Height 3.5m (11ft)
Spread 2m (6½ft)
Interest Distinctive evergreen coniferous tree or shrub

CARE: This plant can be clipped. In colder areas, give more shelter or shade. It is generally free of pests and diseases.

SEQUOIA

Coastal redwood

Sequoia is the tallest living tree in the world and is found naturally in the coastal regions of California and Oregon in the USA. The tallest redwoods are more than 113m (370ft). But don't let this put you off. In the garden they won't grow nearly so tall. A more realistic height is 15–20m (50–65ft). However, what the *Sequoia* does do is grow fast, making a tree 10–15m (33–50ft) in 20 years. They also are one of the few conifers that will reliably coppice if cut down to ground level. Use the natural tree as an evergreen specimen or to form a grove. The cultivar 'Adpressa' is slower growing.

KEY FACTS

Soil Moist to well-drained, can tolerate short term flooding
Site Sun to light shade
Height 4m (13ft)
Spread 2m (6½ft)
Interest Useful for where a tall, evergreen tree is needed quickly

Sequoia sempervirens 'Adpressa'

CARE: No pruning necessary but it will coppice. Can get burnt by cold, dry winds in winter but recovers. No particular problems with pests and diseases.

SEQUOIADENDRON *Wellingtonia*

Also known as big tree and Sierra redwood, this is related to the *Sequoia* (*see* p. 163). *Sequoiadendron* differs from *Sequoia* in having scale-like foliage, cones ripening in the second year and in not being able to coppice. The bark is even thicker but not as soft. It is a hardier tree, not suffering winter cold damage. In the garden, it will make an evergreen specimen tree

20–30m (65–100ft) in height but with a stout trunk. The thick bark is often hollowed by tree creepers and other small birds in winter.

KEY FACTS
Soil Moist to well-drained soil is preferred
Site Full sun
Height 6m (20ft)
Spread 2.5m (8ft)
Interest Excellent but very tall, fast-growing specimen tree with scale-like foliage

Sequoiadendron giganteum

CARE: No pruning necessary. Fast-growing tree. Honey fungus can kill this mighty giant.

SOPHORA

Pagoda tree

This is a large genus of mainly woody plants. The ones in cultivation include two species from the southern hemisphere – *Sophora microphylla* and *Sophora tetraptera* – and one from eastern Asia, *Sophora japonica*. This latter species is now commonly placed in a segregate genus, *Styphnolobium*.

Sophora microphylla and *S. tetraptera* both have small, evergreen leaves composed of many small leaflets, from 10 to 40 pairs. They have yellow flowers in small clusters, carried in late winter or spring. They make shrubs or small trees, to 6m (20ft). *Sophora japonica* is a much taller growing tree, capable of making 20m (67ft) in height and spread.

KEY FACTS

Soil Any well-drained
Site Likes lots of sun
Height 5m (16½ft)
Spread 5m (16½ft)
Interest Elegant leaves, flowers

Sophora microphylla

CARE: No special pruning regime is required, except to reshape or restrain. Relatively trouble-free.

SORBUS

Rowan and whitebeam

Rowans and whitebeams form part of the apple group of the rose family (Rosaceae). They are usually treated as the same genus – *Sorbus* – but botanically this is an artificial genus, comprising several genera that are not closely related. In the strict sense, the generic name *Sorbus* belongs to the rowans.

The other major group included in this genus are the whitebeams. Several smaller groups are also commonly included, particularly the service tree (*Sorbus domestica*) and the wild service tree (*Sorbus torminalis*). If these groups kept themselves to themselves, it would be simple to recognise the

separate genera. However, the majority of them hybridise, apart from *S. domestica*, so it has been common practice to call them all *Sorbus*.

The genus can be characterised by the large clusters of small flowers, from which develop small

Sorbus aucuparia

fruits. The species have three main horticultural attributes: the flowers are showy, mainly in late spring or early summer; in most species the fruits ripen to attractive colours and most give good autumn colour.

Rowan

Rowans (*S. aucuparia*) have red fruits that ripen in midsummer. The autumn colour can be yellow but is not outstanding. Better autumn colour is provided by *Sorbus commixta* and its form 'Embley'. *Sorbus* 'Joseph Rock' is a good tree for restricted space as it has an upright habit. The rowans with white fruits provide much longer-lasting fruits. The best of these will be found in garden centres as *Sorbus hupehensis*, although this name rightly belongs to another species. It makes a small to medium tree roughly 8m (25ft).

Sorbus cashmiriana

Whitebeam

The whitebeams are so-called as they have silvery white undersides to the leaves, and beam is from the Old English word for a tree. The tree that best fits this description is *Sorbus aria*. This makes a dense crowned tree. Even better for foliage is *Sorbus thibetica* 'John Mitchell'; this has large leaves and makes a medium tree with a spreading crown. The Swedish whitebeam, *Sorbus intermedia*, has greyish hairy leaves. Its best attribute is that it is remarkably tough.

KEY FACTS

Soil Well-drained; rowans do best on acidic to neutral; whitebeams thrive on chalk

Site Sun or dappled shade at most

Height 6m (20ft)

Spread 5m (16½ft)

Interest Grown for their ornamental leaves, terminal flowers and mostly spherical berries. Most species also provide good autumn colour

CARE: No specific pruning regime is needed, except to restrict or reshape. Fairly easy to maintain. If grafted, be careful to remove suckers from the root system. Fireblight can cause damage, as can other common diseases but not troubled much by pests.

STEWARTIA
Stuartia

Expect to find this plant in books and nurseries under either *Stewartia* or *Stuartia*. The flowers are white or cream up to 7.5cm (3in) across and carried on short shoots of the current season's growth. Individually the flowers are short-lived but borne in a succession that makes the plant attractive for several weeks over the summer. Autumn colour is also good, mainly yellow or red. The species also has interesting barks; the bark of *Stewartia sinensis* is outstanding – smooth, pink to grey or creamy orange and peels into small translucent coiled strips. Use the plant as a specimen in a moist, light woodland setting or with side shelter.

KEY FACTS
Soil Acidic to neutral, avoid limey soils
Site Sun/dappled shade in moist, sheltered settings
Height 4m (13ft)
Spread 3.5m (11½ft)
Interest Grown for their often peeling bark, simple leaves and cup-shaped flowers

Stewartia malacodendron

CARE: No pruning necessary. *Stewartia* resent being transplanted and are best planted from containers at a small size. Relatively trouble-free.

STYRAX

Storax

This is a large genus of mainly small to medium trees. They are valuable for their massed, medium-sized, bell-shaped flowers that are carried on leafy shoots on last summer's twigs. The flowers are mainly white with yellow anthers – some forms of *Styrax japonicus* have pink flowers. In *S. japonicus* the flowers hang down from the shoots in midsummer. It makes a beautiful small tree. *Styrax obassia* and *S. hemsleyana* have the flowers in large racemes and much larger leaves. They are also taller-growing and are among the best medium-sized summer flowering trees.

Styrax japonicus

KEY FACTS

Soil Acid to neutral, moist but well-drained soil
Site Dappled shade or full sun with side shelter
Height 5m (16½ft)
Spread 4m (13ft)
Interest Bell-shaped flowers

CARE: No special pruning regime required, except to remove defective branches. Plant beside paths where the blooms can be seen both from below and from the side. Does not have any particular problems with pests and diseases.

SYRINGA

Lilac

The lilacs are useful for their fragrant flowers in late spring or early summer. The flowers are carried on new growth made from buds laid down last summer, mainly from the terminal bud.

There are about 20 species but many hybrids, including both single- and double-flowered forms. The common name of the genus is the natural flower colour of *Syringa vulgaris* but a host of other colours have been bred since then, especially whites and purples. Out of flower, they are green and leafy but with no specific beauty and no significant autumn colour. This can be addressed by using them as supports

Syringa vulgaris

for summer climbers such as some *Clematis*, which will not cast too much shade. They can also be underplanted with spring bulbs.

Lilacs can be placed in shrub beds, or can be grown as small specimen trees. They can also be used to make informal hedges, provided that they are trimmed after flowering.

KEY FACTS
Soil Well-drained, especially chalky soils but good on acidic ones
Site Sun or light shade; will not flower satisfactorily in dense shade
Height 3m (10ft)
Spread 2.5m (8ft)
Interest Lilies are mainly grown for their very fragrant flowers

CARE: Remove older wood after flowering. Can be hard pruned to rejuvenate. Avoid spring frost pockets, as late spring frosts can destroy the terminal flower buds. Do not allow suckers from a grafted plant to suppress the desired variety. Lilac blight can affect them, in addition to common problems such as honey fungus.

TAMARIX

Tamarisk

These shrubs and small trees are most often seen in temperate coastal areas, where they really thrive in the windswept, salt-laden climate. Tamarisk has small, almost cypress-like foliage in vigorous sprays and equally small but prolifically carried small pink flowers. In the garden they are excellent in shrub borders or as specimen shrubs or trees. They can also be used to make hedges; if you have a problem from salt spray off a highway in winter, try a hedge of tamarisk instead of the usual cypresses.

KEY FACTS
Soil Well-drained, especially sands
Site Plenty of sun
Height 3m (10ft)
Spread 3m (10ft)
Interest Attractive, feathery foliage
and plume-like small flowers

Tamarix ramosissima

CARE: Unpruned, they tend to become rather straggly. Summer/autumn flowerers – prune as Group 2; spring flowerers – prune after flowering (Group 1) – *see* pp 21–2. Easy to cultivate. In inland situations, they need side shelter from cold, dry winds. Relatively trouble-free.

TAXODIUM

Swamp cypress

Taxodium is a deciduous tree that is superficially similar to *Metasequoia* (see p. 120). In the garden it makes a leafy specimen tree with fresh green summer foliage. It will grow in shallow water and swampy sites, developing special structures, known as 'knees', to get air to the roots. However, fastest growth is on well-drained but moist sites. The leaves have the same combination of deciduous shoots and permanent bud-bearing shoots as *Metasequoia*.

The leaves don't open much before early summer but it is usually late autumn or even early winter before they turn brick red and fall.

KEY FACTS
Soil Swampy to well-drained soil
Site Likes sun
Height 4.5m (4¾ft)
Spread 2m (6½ft)
Interest Upright conical specimen trees with nice foliage that provides good autumn colour

Taxodium distichum

CARE: No pruning necessary but the tree will tolerate it. No particular problems with pests and diseases.

TAXUS

Yew

Yew makes the best hedges of any evergreen. It is generally viewed as slow-growing, but will make a good hedge 2m (6ft) high in five years – only a year slower than the Leyland cypress (*see* p. 70). It can be coppiced or reshaped at any age, quickly sprouting new growth from any branch exposed to the light or from the base. Another advantage is that it does not want to grow taller than 10m (33ft), so does not romp out of control. As an amenity tree, it has lovely habit, foliage and bark. The foliage and bark are poisonous. The aril around the seeds on female trees is the one part not poisonous.

KEY FACTS

Soil Any well-drained soil
Site Sun to deep shade
Height 3.5m (11½ft)
Spread 2m (6½ft)
Interest Peeling bark; attractive habit and foliage. A great hedge plant

Taxus baccata **'Fastigiata'**

CARE: Trim at any time; cut back to ground level. Keep clippings away from animals. Virtually immune to pests and diseases but does not like waterlogging at the roots.

THUJA

Red cedar

This genus has scale-like foliage that is held in flat, spreading sprays. The foliage is delectably scented, often noticeable just by brushing up against the foliage, if not by crushing a small sprig. The cones are small upright structures. *Thuja* makes a vigorous tree that has some live foliage within the crown. This

means that it is much easier to reduce or reshape than the cypresses (*see* p. 70), which have their foliage mainly as a veneer at the edge of the crown (especially in closely trimmed hedges).

Thuja makes an attractive specimen tree, generally wider at the base and conical above. On good sites it can grow to 30m (100ft) or more, but in urban conditions 15–20m (50–65ft) is more likely. The range of tree cultivars is small, with many dwarf ones within *Thuja occidentalis*.

KEY FACTS

Soil Any soil, preferably well-drained, tolerates wet sites; also shallow soils over chalk
Site Would prefer to be situated in a spot with sun or light shade
Height 4m (13ft)
Spread 2m (6½ft)
Interest Scale-like scented foliage; an attractive and vigorous specimen tree that is also suitable for hedging

CARE: Can be lightly pruned provided live foliage remains on any limb. Vigorous evergreens that make good hedges but can grow too large unless carefully trimmed. Red cedar is relatively trouble-free and does not have many problems from pests and diseases.

Thuja plicata 'Zebrina'

THUJOPSIS

Hiba

This tree is related to *Thuja* (*see* p. 176), having similar scale leaves in flattened sprays but without the scent that makes *Thuja* so endearing. The individual scales are shaped like a hatchet, which is the meaning of the Latin name *dolabrata*, and are vividly silvered beneath. It is a slow-growing evergreen, although with time it can make over 15m (50ft). However, in garden settings it is more often a large multi-stemmed shrub and is useful as a small tree in a border. It can be raised from seed but it is easier, and faster, to grow it from cuttings taken in late summer to early winter.

Thujopsis dolabrata

KEY FACTS
Soil Well- to fairly well-drained
Site Sun to moderate shade
Height 4m (13ft)
Spread 1.2m (4ft)
Interest Slow-growing, coniferous evergreen useful in a border

CARE: Tolerates pruning into green/live foliage. It is slow-growing at first. Relatively trouble-free and does not have many problems from pests and diseases.

TILIA

Lime

Limes make large trees. As natural trees, they need large spaces, and most can make 15–25m (50–80ft) in height. There are a few smaller ones, especially the rare *Tilia kiusiana*, which is only a large shrub or small tree to about 6m (20ft). The Mongolian lime, *Tilia mongolica*, is a small tree, usually to around 8m (25ft), and both this and *T. kiusiana* are useful where space is limited. The value of limes lies in their fragrant flowers, which scent the air in midsummer. *Tilia* 'Euchlora' has glossy upper sides to the leaves, but as it ages, it becomes ugly with an untidy mass of lower branches in winter. Far superior are the silver limes (so-called because of the silvery white undersides to their foliage); *Tilia* 'Petiolaris' with its pendent habit is the best of these.

Limes can be raised from seed, which will usually germinate in the second spring. The varieties are usually grafted onto seedling rootstocks; they can also be layered.

CARE: Prune to restrict growth; they are very tolerant of severe pruning so try annual or biennial pollarding. Large-growing trees, some produce a mass of honeydew and basal suckers. Aphids can affect some varieties; also a rust fungus can lead to leaf fall in early autumn.

KEY FACTS

Soil Will grow in any well-drained soil type

Site This plant prefers a position that is in sun or light shade

Height 7m (23ft)

Spread 4m (13ft)

Interest Limes are grown for their stately habit, foliage and fragrant flowers, which are followed by dry, nut-like fruits

Tilia 'Petiolaris'

TOONA

Chinese mahogany

This genus is represented in cultivation by *Toona sinensis*. The foliage is large and pinnate, giving a bold appearance. The terminal leaflet is often missing, meaning that the leaf has an even number of leaflets.

The new foliage of *Toona* is edible and has an oniony flavour. In Beijing it is grown for this purpose, rather than for the fragrant white flowers that are produced in midsummer, or the yellow autumn colour. In the garden, *Toona sinensis* 'Flamingo' is especially attractive in early summer with its brilliant pink new foliage. Use it as a specimen tree.

KEY FACTS

Soil Fertile and well-drained soil
Site Full sun
Height 5m (16½ft)
Spread 2m (6½ft)
Interest Fragrant summer flowers, good autumn colour and edible foliage

Toona sinensis 'Flamingo'

CARE: No pruning required, except to reshape or restrict. *Toona sinensis* 'Flamingo' is best with sun shining through its foliage. Relatively trouble-free.

TROCHODENDRON

This genus contains only a single species that is unique as a broadleaved tree in having the wood characteristics of a conifer. The foliage looks a bit like ivy (*Hedera*). It makes a slow-growing, evergreen bush, although with time it can make a tree. The flowers are vivid green, very distinctive and useful for flower arrangements. It appears tender but is actually very tough, especially if given some side shelter. In the garden it is useful as an evergreen tree (or large shrub) in a border or in a woodland garden area.

Trochodendron aralioides

KEY FACTS

Soil Acidic to neutral soil, not over chalk
Site This plant enjoys sun to moderate shade
Height 2.5m (8ft)
Spread 2m (6½ft)
Interest Distinctive vivid spring/summer flowers and handsome leaves

CARE: No pruning required, except to reshape or restrict. Thrives with side shelter. Relatively trouble-free and does not have any particular problems with pests and diseases.

TSUGA

Hemlock

Tsuga heterophylla is one of the most beautiful of all evergreen trees. Young trees are narrowly conical in shape with slightly pendent branches that carry the dense green foliage with silvery undersides. The leading shoot is nodding, giving a graceful aspect to the tree. Older trees are broader but where they have sufficient side light, retain the foliage down to ground level.

As a free-growing specimen tree, *Tsuga* is hard to beat. It is very shade tolerant and can be used in dark shady corners. It can also be used to make attractive hedges.

KEY FACTS

Soil Well- to fairly well-drained; good on dry, acidic sands
Site Sun to moderate shade
Height 2m (6½ft)
Spread 2m (6½ft)
Interest A beautiful, coniferous evergreen; specimen tree or hedge

Tsuga heterophylla

CARE: Can be pruned if there is sufficient live foliage. In open sites *Tsuga* can get damaged by spring frosts when young. Relatively trouble-free otherwise.

ULMUS

Elm

The advent in the late 1960s of the aggressive strain of Dutch elm disease has reduced the appearance of elms significantly, particularly in parts of Europe. Still elms are excellent trees, tolerant of salt spray and exposure, and a wide range of soil types. Some modern hybrids are not affected by the disease but these are not widely planted. Wych elm (*Ulmus glabra*) is still frequently planted, as is the smooth-leaved elm (*Ulmus minor*). The former is the only elm to reproduce by seed. But the majestic trees of *Ulmus procera* (English elm) are now replaced by short-lived suckers, making perhaps 12m (39ft) before succumbing to infection.

Ulmus minor
'Dampieri Aurea'

KEY FACTS

Soil Well-drained to heavy soils, acidic to alkaline
Site Sun to light shade
Height 6m (20ft)
Spread 4m (13ft)
Interest Grown as specimens. Flowers in spring, fruits appear in summer

CARE: No pruning required but tolerant of heavy pruning. *Ulmus* is susceptible to Dutch elm disease.

UMBELLULARIA *California or Oregon laurel*

The common name depends upon whether you are in California or Oregon! This relative of the bay laurel (*see* p. 105) makes an attractive evergreen tree. The yellow flowers are followed by the purple fruits, which contain a single seed.

The foliage is strongly and attractively fragrant; resist sniffing for too long as the volatile component will give a splitting headache half an hour or so later. The volatile oil in the foliage is also reported to have given some people dermatitis. In the garden it makes an attractive evergreen that is colourful in spring.

KEY FACTS
Soil Well-drained soil
Site Prefers to grow in sun to light shade
Height 4m (13ft)
Spread 2.5m (8ft)
Interest Good specimen tree with spring flowers and autumn fruits

Umbellularia californica

CARE: No pruning required but tolerant of heavy pruning. Fairly trouble-free from pests and diseases.

WISTERIA

This genus is naturally a climber, quick-growing and capable of making 6m (20ft) in a year. It is excellent for growing into and through tall trees. It also tolerates both acidic and alkaline soils. As wisteria can grow into a 20m (67ft) tree, forget pruning at that height and just enjoy the flowers! It is only the current season's growth that is flexible and wand-like. It can also easily be trained to form a free-standing shrub.

KEY FACTS

Soil Will grow in any well-drained soil
Site Full sun
Height 10m (33ft)
Spread 10m (33ft)
Interest Showy, fragrant, pea-like flowers in spring

Wisteria floribunda

CARE: There are no particular problems from pests and diseases.

ZELKOVA

This genus is related to the elms (*see* p. 184) but is much less at risk of Dutch elm disease and has a small drupe (*see* p. 146) instead of the winged fruit found in elms. The leaves are small and turn yellow through to orange-brown/ red in autumn; unlike the leaves of elms, they are symmetrical at the base. The bark is smooth and grey but small flakes exfoliate to reveal an orange inner bark. In the garden, they make imposing specimen trees, although they can be trimmed to keep them small.

KEY FACTS
Soil Well-drained soils; both acidic and alkaline
Site Sun to light shade
Height 5m (16½ft)
Spread 5m (16½ft)
Interest Imposing specimen tree with attractive foliage, which provides good autumn colour, and interesting bark

Zelkova serrata

CARE: No pruning needed – the plant is very easy to look after. It can get Dutch elm disease but only in an epidemic.

INDEX

If you have enjoyed this book, why not build on your expertise with other Collins titles?

Fill your garden with drama and dimension – successfully choose, plant and care for the most popular varieties of architectural plants
192pp
£4.99
PB   0 00 720124 9

The definitive book on cultivating flowering shrubs, for all amateur and intermediate gardeners
160pp
£6.99
PB   0 00 714653 1

From planning and design to selecting plants and garden maintenance, the only garden book you'll ever need
336pp
£15.99
PB   0 00 719184 7

Packed with projects for getting kids involved in the garden
128pp
£14.99
HB   0 00 719311 4

To order any of these titles please telephone **0870 787 1732**
For further information about Collins books visit our website: **www.collins.co.uk**

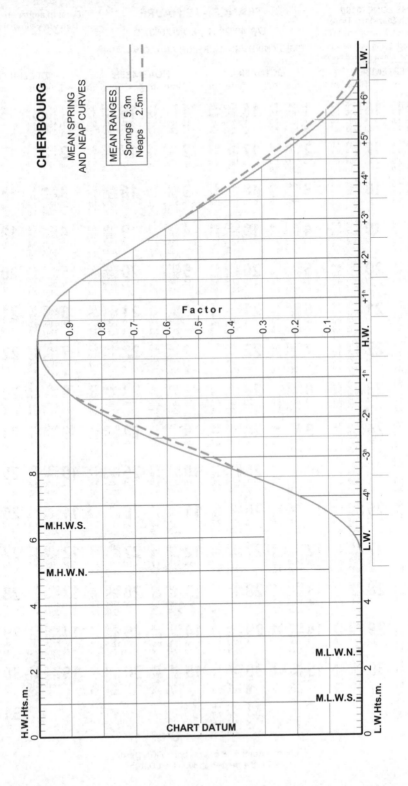

CHERBOURG

MEAN SPRING
AND NEAP CURVES

MEAN RANGES
Springs 5.3m
Neaps 2.5m